Building Resilience: A Peer Coaching Manual

Assisting Others to Acquire and Sustain Positive Change

By

Ronald L. Breazeale, Ph.D.
Richard C. Lumb, Ph.D.

June 29, 2020

To Rob, a man who brings honor to veterans, community, and self. Your commitment and dedication to helping others overcome and refocus on their life bring peace, forgiving, and a new direction. Critical elements as we navigate through the time we are given.

Breham

Cover design by Rosalba Breazeale
http://www.rosalbabreazeale.com/

Index

Chapter	Page

---

[1] . *The Resilience Coaches Manual is not intended to be a substitute for professional medical advice for which your healthcare professional is your best source.*

Preface

This manual is premised on the assumption that there is no single most effective model of helping people when conditions, situations, or events occur to upset balance in life. We know the impact of stress, adversity, and trauma is often left to work itself out. But at what cost? Usually, an event occurs that disrupts normal life and forces the individual to refocus in a different way of trying to resolve the problem. Finding a path around the obstacles encountered is often too daunting to consider. We need not go it alone when faced with a negative experience, especially when associates are trained to assist us. We can move forward to a return to balance more quickly when we are supported.

Science and practice have identified steps that can be taken by the individual or by others with whom they work, live, or associate to resolve problems that may seem unresolvable at first.

Society besieged by all manner of negativity including political and economic uncertainty that can contribute to a pessimistic attitude in our lives. Ignoring these realities is not the answer. Learning to be resilient in

Noticing that something is wrong often triggers a belief that time will heal all things and we ignore what is happening. As a friend, colleague, or supervisor, it may be appropriate to seek to help that person. Refusal is always an option by the person, but often assistance is welcomed, if approached correctly and with the proper intent.

the face of adversity can be. We hope to increase your interest and skill in resilience coaching

In this manual information and tools are provided to guide your interest in acquiring the skills of a resilience coach, a person who will reach out to help others. If the decision to engage is made, do so with clear intent, knowledge, and sincerity and concern for the other person. Saving lives is not always an emergency room endeavor, it often is personal, one on one, where caring and willingness to assist another person, shines brightly through the gloom of discouragement and despair.
Intended Audience:

Audiences vary with time and circumstances:

- Emergency Services Personnel
- School Officials and Teachers
- Those you work with
- As a supervisor of others
- A friend, family member or colleague
- Business and Manufacturing Organizations
- Volunteer Organizations and Groups
- Veterans

Authors

Ronald L. Breazeale, Ph.D.

Breazeale received his doctorate in clinical psychology from the University of Tennessee in 1974.Dr. Breazeale is a clinical psychologist with over 30 years of experience in the fields of mental health and alcohol and drug abuse. Dr. Breazeale has developed and administered numerous mental health and substance abuse programs in hospitals, mental health centers, and independent group practices. These have included Criminal Justice Liaison Programs, Emergency Services, and Specialized Outpatient Service Programs. Dr. Breazeale has served as the Executive Director for Psychological and Educational Services, the most extensive independent group mental health and substance abuse practice in Northern New England. He has been active in the field of professional psychology, serving as President of the Maine Psychological Association and was instrumental in the formation of the Maine Division of Independent Practice. He has served on the Council of Representatives of the American Psychological Association and was involved in the establishment of APA's Psychology Rural Health Interest Group.

Dr. Breazeale has worked with public safety organization in some capacities since the mid-1970. He assisted in the development of a program for public safety supervisors and managers to recognize employee issues and problems and devise strategies to address them before they became a significant concern. This program taught by the Carolinas Institute for Community Policing, a project funded by the Department of Justice, Office of Community Oriented Policing, and Washington, D.C. His project, "Building Resilience...Survival Skills for the 21st. Century" collaborated with the American Red Cross of Maine, Emergency Management Agencies, and Alpha One. Resilience training for public safety personnel is one of its focus areas; providing skills to help manage crises, reduce everyday stressful situations, and be more effective in meeting job and personal demands associated with daily living. Website: *http://building-resilience.com*.

Dr. Breazeale is the author of a series of novels that help to conquer fear, build resilience and bounce back from adversity. They are: "Reaching Home," "First Night," and "Starjacked." They have become the core material in the resilience training programs that he and his colleagues, in Building Resilience, utilize in their training. He has also worked with his colleagues in developing BounceBack, a serious game used as a training tool in teaching resilience skills.

Areas of consultation expertise for Dr. Breazeale include crisis intervention and management, assessment and management of potentially violent situations, public safety psychology, rural healthcare, managed care system development and the management of disabling illnesses and chronic conditions. Dr. Breazeale is currently working with Pocket Confidant as they develop and utilize artificial intelligence to provide resilience coaching.

Richard C. Lumb, Ph.D.

Lumb received his doctorate from Florida State University, and his Master and bachelor's degrees from the University of Southern Maine. Lumb's academic career includes:

Chair and Program Director of Criminal Justice and Police Certification Training at Western Piedmont Community College, in Morganton, North Carolina. In that role, he was also Director of the Western North Carolina Basic Law Enforcement Training Program for WPCC. WPCC also provided an active continuing professional development program for area police and sheriffs.

Additionally, Associate Professor, Department of Criminal Justice at the University of North Carolina at Charlotte. Associate Professor and Graduate Coordinator, Department of Criminal Justice at Northern Michigan University. Later, Chair and Associate Professor, Department of Criminal Justice, the State University of New York at Brockport. He developed and managed the Institute for Leadership Development (ILD) at SUNY Brockport and the Institute for Public Safety Policy Studies.

Lumb has over twenty-eight years of direct police service and overall, fifty-four years' experience in the criminal justice and public safety system. He served with the Maine State Police, Chief of Police in Old Orchard Beach Maine, and as Chief of Police and Fire at the Morganton Department of Public Safety in Morganton, North Carolina. While completing his doctorate at Florida State University, Lumb worked for the Tallahassee Police Department, Tallahassee, Florida as Director of the E-911 Center and Community Officer Program.

As an Associate Professor in the Department of Criminal Justice at the University of North Carolina at Charlotte, he was also the Director of the Research, Planning and Analysis Bureau at the Charlotte-Mecklenburg Police Department, under an agreement between the University and the City of Charlotte. Lumb wrote the grant that funded the Carolinas Institute for Community Policing, a project funded by United States Department of Justice, Office of Community Oriented Policing Services. Lumb served as Director of the CICP for over five years.

At Charlotte-Mecklenburg Police Department, Lumb was responsible for Geographic Information Systems (GIS) analysis (crime and problem-solving analysis that included spatial and temporal GIS mapping), policy development, program development, and evaluation, assisting field units with problem-solving initiatives, assisted District Captains, Command Staff and citizens with crime and social disorder problem resolutions. The CMPD was fully vested in the Community Problem Oriented Policing (CPOP) model with extreme emphasis on building police and community partnerships, including both public and private organizations. Lumb worked directly with Dr. Herman Goldstein (the originator of Community Problem Oriented Policing - CPOP) and Dr. Ronald Clarke (author of Crime Prevention Through Environmental Design - CPTED) for eighteen months.

He was an evaluator of "Crisis Intervention Training" provided to County Jails by NAMI Maine and worked with Southern Maine Community College as a contractor on the Maine Department of Corrections project. In that role, he directed the SMCC's Criminal Justice Initiatives, providing education and professional development, conducting research, program planning, and evaluation and other services to Maine communities and public safety agencies.

During his policing career, Lumb was the recipient of the <u>Second Annual J. Edgar Hoover Award</u> for contributions to the professionalization of law enforcement. He served in several community organizations including two-term Board Chairman of the York County Counseling Services and Chairman of the Governor's Mental Health Advisory Council in the State of Maine.

Contributors to this manuscript:

Charlene Fernald Moynihan
Maurice Namwira
Alphonse Ndayikengurukiye
Isla Reddin
Rita Schiano

CHAPTER One
What is Resilience?

A. What is Resilience Coaching?

Coaching is about change. The coach can help you set goals and assist in working through the obstacles that inhibit you from reaching them. A coach assists you make a positive difference in areas of your life, such as work-related issues, relationships, health issues, and to manage life events like job loss or to sort out complex problems, assisting in determining the best path forward.

Resilience is the power to adapt well to adversity. It is the process of coping with and managing tragedy and crisis. It is "bouncing back" from the difficulty that impacts well-being. Examples are national disasters such as hurricanes or terrorist attacks, wildfires, and weather and other natural events resulting in destruction. There are personal disasters; examples are bankruptcy, divorce, or the death of a loved one.

Research since the New York City twin tower attack suggests that resilience may be much more common than we thought. Although specific forms of temperament may be inherited and may help people to be more resilient in a crisis, and although types of psychiatric or cognitive disorders such as schizophrenia may interfere with the learning of these skills; most of what makes up resilience is learned and easily taught to others. This is especially true with one critical component of resilience; optimism.

Being resilient does not mean we see the world through rose-colored glasses, avoiding pain or experiencing intense emotions when going through a crisis. It is just the opposite. Resilient individuals are aware of their feelings and can discharge and manage them, even while dealing with and leading others in a crisis. Resilience does not involve avoiding one's feelings; it consists in confronting and maintaining them. Being able to think clearly and control one's emotions is a significant part of resilience.

For example, preparing for a natural disaster or another socially disabling event, applies pre-planning and preparation, utilizing many resilience skills to include realistic planning, taking steps to ensure communications  with outside people and groups, food, shelter, and other essential life needs. While most disasters are of short duration, we must be able to continue life, utilizing our skills and knowledge, until normalcy is restored.

Situations that negatively impact a person, require forethought and planning. We need a variety of strategies to assist us to emerge quickly and with diminished lingering trauma. An emergency kit to address the effects of stress, adversity and trauma include occasional intervention from a peer, someone trained in coaching others to find pathways to balance.

B. Why Should We Teach/Coach Others in Building Resilience?

Experts anticipate the likelihood of another 911 event in the future. Simple planning for that eventuality allows us to be more resilience, should we encounter such an event. Where we live, the environment and demographics can impact our resilience. The Federal Emergency Management Agency, State, County and local municipalities all have plans in place; becoming familiar with them helps to increase personal and family resilience.

Some countries have developed reasonably elaborate programs in assessment and training in resilience. They have defined resilience both as the resilience of the citizenry of their country as well as its infrastructure. Unfortunately, many of us in the U.S. have slipped back into believing that there will not be another 911. History demonstrates that natural and human-made disasters occur far too frequently, an understanding that demands consideration.

Whether we believe that there will be another 911- as an event, we would all agree that there will be natural disasters. History provides numerous examples, and we can anticipate more in the future. Hurricanes, ice storms, floods, and tornados are expected to be more frequent in the immediate future. And, other threats loom on the horizon including terrorism, pandemics, more powerful weather storms, and events to which we have little control such as an earthquake.

Perhaps you have never been affected by a natural disaster, nor anticipate it happening. This outcome is real for many of us. However, globally there have been many examples of personal tragedies.

We know that resilience skills and concepts developed through research can be learned and applied to our and the lives of others. Knowledge of resilience can assist individuals in being able to adapt to and survive difficult times.

Training in resilience reduces the frequency and intensity of post-traumatic stress disorders and other health problems that occur after experiencing an unusual event. Training allows society, families, and individuals impacted by disaster to recover more quickly. Reinforcing individual coping skills increases the likelihood they will demonstrate resilience and not be overwhelmed by an unusual event.

We know that the skills and concepts developed through research on resilience can be learned and applied and can assist individuals in being more able to adapt to and survive difficult times.

We know that people who have difficulty managing their emotions, specifically fear, become more restrained and rigid in their views and less able to envision the bigger picture. A "circle-the-wagons" mentality increases paranoia and often results in a narrowing of perception. An example result is the rejection and persecution of those who are different illustrated by their religion, race, sexual preference or physical or mental ability. Witness our society's reaction to these groups during the years since the September 11th terrorist attack in New York City.

Reacting emotionally, rather than careful thinking and rational problem-solving often results in decisions made through fear. These decisions can negatively affect others and are later regretted. Defending society and culture is an inclusive rather than an exclusive process. We should seek alliances, cooperative problem-solving, sustainable community collaboration building, and consensus regarding future actions.

We must invest in strengthening personal resilience. It includes support for building resilience in our family members, friends, and other members of society.

C. What Factors Make Resilient People?

Research demonstrates that individuals manage adversity in multiple ways. The different approaches and strategies used have been shaped by culture, social norms, and family customs they acquired. They all have common factors of similarity.

1. <u>Being able to connect and communicate with others</u>. Relationships that provide support and care are one of the primary factors in resilience. Having a number of these relationships, both within and

outside of the family, that offer love, encouragement, and reassurance can build and support resilience (e.g., developing new friendships).

2. <u>The ability to be flexible</u>. Flexibility is a critical component of resilience and one of the primary factors in emotional adjustment and maturity. Flexibility requires that an individual is accommodating in their thinking and actions (e.g., trying something new).

3. <u>Problem-solve both individually and with others</u>. Make realistic plans and act to carry them out. Understanding what is (reality) rather than what you want it to be, is part of this skill. It also requires being proactive rather than reactive and assertive not aggressive or passive. These are components of this skill (e.g., plan to save others by taking a Red Cross course in CPR and First Aid).

4. <u>The ability to manage strong feelings</u>. It is the ability to set emotions to the side when clear thinking is needed. The ability to utilize clear thinking to manage your feelings is a vital component of this skill (e.g., when you're angry or hurt; think before acting).

5. <u>Being self-confident</u>. Retaining a positive self-image is critical to confronting and managing fear and anxiety in one's life. It is the ability to manage obstacles that might prevent you from moving forward with your goals. (e.g., believe in your ability to deal with setbacks).

6. <u>Being able to find meaning and purpose</u>. The ability to make sense of what is occurring and to find the meaning of it is critical if we want to manage the

feelings that emerge in a crisis. Spiritual and religious practices are often a component of this factor (e.g., act on your values).

7. <u>Being able to see the big picture</u>. Optimists generally can understand the bigger picture, more so than pessimists. Optimists are more likely to discern good and bad events occurring in their life as a temporary condition rather than a permanent one. They see events as having a specific impact on specific aspects of their life, rather than a persistent impact on their future. And last, of all, they are less likely to blame themselves or someone else for the adverse event. Optimists avoid the blame game (e.g., hold yourself and others accountable without blaming.)

8. <u>The ability to appreciate and use humor</u>. Laughter may have healing powers. Find the humor when you might otherwise be left with negative thoughts and/or emotions.

9. <u>Caring for oneself</u>. Take care of your physical and emotional needs. Eat regularly, exercise, play games/a sport. Being your best requires feeling your best.

10. <u>The ability to care for others</u>. Practice what you have learned, share your skills with others. Occupations and volunteer activities that involve caring for others can often build resilience.

<u>Ten skills and attitudes that are characteristic of resilient people.</u>

1. Connect and communicate with others.
2. Be flexible.
3. Problem solve.

4. Manage strong feelings.
5. Self-confidence.
6. Find meaning and purpose.
7. See the big picture.
8. Appreciate and use humor.
9. Care for yourself.
10. Care for others.

D. Teaching Resilience Building Through Storytelling

Reaching Home (Breazeale, 2019), is a novel about fear and resilience. It raises the question of what society will do if we are attacked again. Based loosely on Terror Management Theory, the story is set in the not-too-distant future, the year 2023. The main character, Lee, transcends the typical notions of how heroes look and act. He has never made peace with the South growing up in as a child without a left hand, with the prosthetic hook that he wears, and the nuclear industry he blames for his disability. He returns to the Southeast to research material for a book that he is writing. While there, an explosion occurs in one of the DOE plants, and Lee is caught up in the ensuing disaster and implicated in what is mistakenly believed to be a terrorist plot. He manages to escape the local authorities. Much of the story focuses on his journey back to Maine and the unlikely allies he meets along the way. Now on the radar of federal agents tracking a terrorist cell in Boston, Lee is arrested before he can reach home. He is offered a deal: Help the FBI foil the plot and avoid prosecution. To reach home, Lee must confront his fears and question his perceptions of good and evil. There are no superheroes in this story. People with disabilities in this story – and there are them – are ordinary people living their lives as best they can. They have all the blemishes and the vices of the average person, as well as the courage and strength that all human beings possess.

So why use a novel like <u>Reaching Home</u> to teach people about resilience and disability? Teaching through storytelling has been around since the first humans told stories about their lives. These first training sessions on resilience occurred thousands of year ago. From campfires to fireplaces to pot-bellied stoves to water coolers, we continue to tell stories about resilience. In more recent times, we have written this down in the form of novels or biographies, and even more recently recorded them on tape and film, and most recently on the Internet.

But a story, I would argue, is one of the best ways to teach the concepts and skills involved in resilience. The average person requires 12 to 14 hours to complete a novel. This time is often spread over weeks or months and in the late evening before falling asleep. The activity is usually enjoyable, with the reader frequently identifying with one or more of the characters in the story. It is for all these reasons that I believe that a novel like <u>Reaching Home</u> is an ideal vehicle, far better than lectures, textbooks or brochures, to teach the concepts and introduce the skills and attitudes of resilience. A Resilience Trilogy, which consists of Reaching Home and two other novels by Dr. Breazeale, Starjacked and First Night, is also a resource for teaching these skills.

"The faces of the police and first responders provide a window to the internal world of feelings and emotions, and when they encounter adversity or exposure to danger, trauma, and other adverse job-related events, they present a mask of determination, and strength and endurance. The event has summoned the officer, and he or she has responded and must now take charge, bring order to disorder, confront danger with their training, and often endure as a silent witness to yet another human tragedy. No tears will fall at what is observed. No emotion must be witnessed, and the physiological and psychological systems of the officer will instantly achieve full power as anticipation, safety, and decisions are made at light speed. The officer's senses are sharpened, eyes observe what is rapidly taking place, smells and sounds are acute, movement and behavior of people are perceived and mentally recorded, and the officer's body is tense as the high output of adrenalin is pumped throughout the body. A state of high readiness is taking place, automatic and in response to perceived danger. The individual officer is not thinking of anything else except what is within the immediate vicinity, determining

*next steps, adapting protective
action from a potential threat, and
developing a response to address
the issue or emergency that they
cannot choose to avoid (Lumb,
2013).*

*In the officer's head, the neurons
that connect the prefrontal lobes of
the brain resting just behind the
forehead, surging tides of thought
and feelings are blasting forth into
consciousness. The intellect, located
in the neocortex a more recently
evolved layer at the top of the
brain, is contacting the ancient
subcortex, located lower and more
rooted in the mind. The reception
and processing of information lead
to decisions and evokes an
emotional response. When danger
is encountered and where harm or
death could result, the natural fight
or flight syndrome flashes red,
signaling an immediate need for
action. Adrenalin surges giving the
person extreme energy and
awareness for a short time, and as
it wears down, fatigue backfills
leaving the individual exhausted.
The emotion of fear elicits caution
and awareness. Feelings of
happiness, comfort and other
thoughts are shut down due to the
heightened awareness of
unusualness and the need for full*

attention to what is being confronted.

Facial expressions, voice pitch and tone, body language and other perceptible manifestations indicate the need to control, to take charge, and to bring order to chaos. The officer's sweat glands are overproducing. His or her heart is beating faster, and more rapid and shallow breaths are taken as the stress of the moment maintains heightened awareness and a sense of protection, warning, and potential for danger. The officer's training kicks in and many automatic reactions will occur - all within the proper bounds of what has been instilled into a response being determined.

And, when it is over, the body seeks to return to normal. There is often a feeling of fatigue, sometimes disbelief, anger, hunger and the need to be around others who can understand what was just experienced. When officers have gathered to sit and wind down at the end of high-stress events, they often resort to retelling the stories of what just happened. They emphasize exciting events, points of danger, observations and feelings toughened by exposure; often these

retellings are laced with
descriptions of perps as "assholes,"
"motherfuckers" and other
descriptors that indicate the disdain
and disgust they are feeling.
Reliving and reviewing the event
help with the understanding of
what remains a blurry event.

Talking also helps to reduce the
stress and elicit support from
others, this, like a pressure cooker
relief valve, allows the heightened
inner emotions to slowly return to
normal. It is at this moment the
officer is acutely aware of feelings
that will range from the need to cry
to extreme exhilaration and real or
simulated anger. Frequently, the
officer or group will retire to a local
"cops bar" where the stories are
retold along with consumption of
alcohol, the medication of choice. If
a spouse or other family share the
officer's life, they will typically not
be present for these events. Not
sharing gives both parties reason to
distance themselves from one
another. Often this is not done
consciously. But it effectively builds
barriers that are difficult to
surmount. The gap tends to grow,
spreading outward in gradual
decay until one finds the chasm too
wide to cross anymore.

A freight train of emotion occurred, and it took away a substantial piece of normalcy. In its wake is left a subtle layer of stress that will not diminish by itself. As time passes and numerous similar situations occur, the layer deepens, and the trauma encountered, often adds to the damage. We often see the results manifesting themselves in harmful ways. When compared with the average population, police and police and first responder's officers experience a higher rate of a heart ailment, over-weight, excessive use of alcohol or drugs, relationship problems, and social atrophy. Also, there are elevated levels of anger and distrust that rule the head and heart. None of which is healthy (Williams and Huber, 1986).

The organization that one works for provides the physical body protection from harm with vests, guns, pepper spray, handcuffs, and other equipment. Rarely is there a career-long plan to address the emotional or cognitive side. The long-term outcome of this neglect is often reflected by higher than average early death, suicide, physical and mental illness – signs of deterioration and a lifetime of traumatic encounters not

*adequately addressed. There is a
withering of life that has stripped
away any chance for healthy
longevity in a post-career lifestyle."*

Examples in life are teaching moments. We experience the plight of others and make a comparison to our lives; we re-live some of them through the readings. We must also find solutions, pathways to positive change, including a return to optimism and wellbeing. If we do not, we are doomed to residing in the negativity of the situation that we want to change.

E. *BounceBack*: A Peer Coaching Tool.

We love storytelling. It has been around for as long as we humans have. We watch stories unfold on T.V., in the movies, and on social media. We read stories in books and magazines. We listen as stories are told in song, on talk radio and by friends, family, and co-workers. Why do we love it so? Because stories may be entertaining and amusing, informative and educational. Empathy stirs. We engage emotionally. Our minds are stimulated as we follow a sequence of events that leads us to question, "How would I have responded had it been my story?"

Stories allow us to connect with the characters, to flex our cognitive muscle and problem solve. Sometimes we relate to the humor while experiencing the sadness at others. We ask ourselves, how would I have taken care of myself? Would I have cared for others? Some readers will dig even deeper, wondering what personal values would have dictated my behavior/actions and how much importance any of it has in the big picture.

BounceBack is a serious game, a tool to help build mental toughness by asking people to respond to real-world challenges, using the Skills & Attitudes of resilience. Storytelling is a powerful tool and BounceBack presents snippets of stories that users learn from. It's a deck of cards that consists of 20 Challenge cards and 10 Skills & Attitudes cards per deck. Each deck addresses issues such as disability, poverty, and immigration.

Each deck focusses on challenges faced by particular people. People of differing race, color, religion, national origin, socioeconomic standing, sexual orientation, occupation/vocation and state of physical/mental health to name a few. How do we know what challenges are faced by whom? By listening to the stories of others who have offered to share them with us.

Not all challenges are unique to only one individual/community, but there are some that are. Police officers, immigrants and those who live in poverty certainly face challenges unique to their situation. While not quite as unique, there are challenges relevant to ones' age. Adolescents and teens face a different set of challenges than Baby Boomers do. Individuals with health/mental health concerns may share similar problems related to illness and yet still have unique challenges directly associated with their condition(s). What we provide by creating many decks, is something that speaks universally to the need to empathize with unfamiliar others and the need for a coaching/teaching tool that speaks directly to some of those unique challenges that are difficult to discuss and even harder to navigate.

There are many ways to use BounceBack. As stated previously, each deck contains a set of Challenge Cards and a set of Skills & Attitudes cards. The Skills & Attitudes cards are used to respond to the scenarios on the Challenge Cards. Here's how it works. You're presented with a Challenge Card. Spread the ten Skills & Attitudes cards out so that they can be seen and read them over.

Ten Skills & Attitudes that can help build resilience:

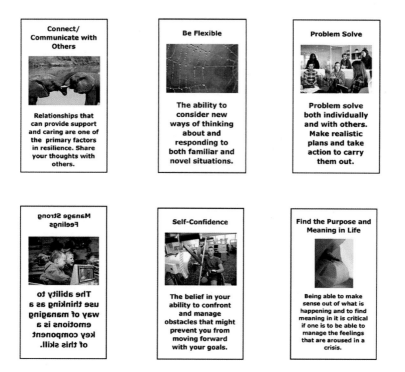

See the Big Picture

Look beyond the immediate situation with optimism. Consider the impact before locking in your response. Positivity encourages better outcomes.

Appreciate and use Humor

Laughter may have healing powers. Find the humor when you might otherwise be left with negative thoughts and/or emotions.

Care for Yourself

Take care of your physical and emotional needs. Eat regularly, exercise, play games/a sport. Being your best requires feeling your best.

Care for Others

Practice what you have learned, share your skills with others. Occupations and volunteer activities that involve caring for others can often build resilience.

Read the challenge on the face of the first card presented. Here are some examples:

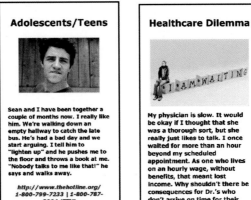

Adolescents/Teens

Sean and I have been together a couple of months now. I really like him. We're walking down an empty hallway to catch the late bus. He's had a bad day and we start arguing. I tell him to "lighten up" and he pushes me to the floor and throws a book at me. "Nobody talks to me like that!" he says and walks away.

http://www.thehotline.org/
1-800-799-7233 | 1-800-787-3224 (TTY)

Healthcare Dilemma

My physician is slow. It would be okay if I thought that she was a thorough sort, but she really just likes to talk. I once waited for more than an hour beyond my scheduled appointment. As one who lives on an hourly wage, without benefits, that meant lost income. Why shouldn't there be consequences for Dr.'s who don't arrive on time for their appointments?

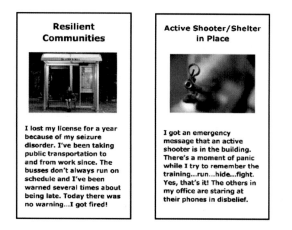

Resilient Communities

I lost my license for a year because of my seizure disorder. I've been taking public transportation to and from work since. The busses don't always run on schedule and I've been warned several times about being late. Today there was no warning...I got fired!

Active Shooter/Shelter in Place

I got an emergency message that an active shooter is in the building. There's a moment of panic while I try to remember the training...run...hide...fight. Yes, that's it! The others in my office are staring at their phones in disbelief.

Using the ten cards previously viewed, select the cards having the Skills & Attitudes you wish to apply to manage the challenge at hand. When we say ask we mean not only choosing the Skills & Attitudes that you feel might help but sharing the specifics of how they would be implemented.

- Who would you connect/communicate with and why?
- How would you demonstrate flexibility?
- Would your problem be solved alone or with others and why?
- How would you manage your strong feelings?
- How can you muster self-confidence?
- What values do you hold that lend meaning to the challenge and what is driving your response to the challenge?

- How much importance does the challenge have compared to the big picture and how is this driving your response?
- If humor is an option, how would apply it and with whom?
- How exactly would you care for yourself?
- How and why would you care for others?

Repeat this process, in turn, for each participant. Don't forget the discussion. Sharing thoughts is part of the learning process. Perhaps the most valuable part of the experience. The goal is to bring people together to share thoughts and perspectives on how to respond to the many chalienge's life puts forth.

BounceBack was developed as a tool to practice responding to real-life challenges. Challenges are presented, and the user chooses Skills and Attitudes that he or she wishes to apply to respond to that challenge. It's effortless. It's practice. With >37 decks and >740 challenge questions, it's a lot of practice. The beauty of BounceBack is that it is simple and adaptable. It can be used alone, with a peer or in a small group. It can be used by a coach with an individual or in a classroom. It can be used by business to build more resilient employees. We provide the challenges; you decide how to use them best.

For peer coaching, you may want to present a single Challenge Card to a diverse group of people. Have them each draw a Skills & Attitudes card and share how they would apply the card drawn to the challenge presented. Another approach might be to have each participant draw their Challenge Card and take turns sharing the Skills & Attitudes each would apply to the challenge card drawn.

Bringing two divergent groups together for coaching/learning from one another is another option. Think about groups in your community that might interact more productively if they had a better understanding of the challenges faced by each.

Healthcare providers and their patients, police officers and the community members they serve might be a few examples. Choose BounceBack decks that address the issues to be discussed by the groups.

In the first example, the decks that would be useful are Healthcare Professional and Healthcare Dilemma. The former addresses challenges faced by medical providers and the latter by patients. The First Responder/Public Safety deck addresses challenges faced by police officers and first responders. Multiple decks address possible community descriptors such as Immigrants, The 13.5% (poverty) and Rank and File (middle class). Utilizing this example, the idea is to have the police officers draw challenges from, let's say, Immigrants and the immigrants draw challenges from the First Responder/Public Safety deck. Participants would be attempting to apply the Skills & Attitudes of resilience to less familiar challenges.

Since we are talking about a potentially large group of people, it makes some sense to have the group respond (rather than individuals) to the challenges drawn. As a group, say, police officers, have them select as many Skills & Attitudes that they wish to apply and share them with the other group, let's say, immigrants. The immigrants would coach officers by providing feedback on the proposed responses to the challenge presented and vice versa. Sharing one's experience with successful responses to common challenges with those who do not have the value of that experience not only builds a deeper understanding of one another but facilitates the learning. New Skills & Attitudes can become a part of an improved response repertoire.

The questions below are designed to elicit thoughts and feelings in response to a challenge. They relate to the 10 Skills and Attitudes of resilience. These Skills & Attitudes may need development to help individuals respond to challenges, move towards their self-chosen life goals and achieve the balance that will allow him/her to feel fulfilled even as life continually demands change.

- Feelings are an emotional state or reaction. What are the feelings you have as a result of drawing this challenge?
- On a scale of 1-5 (1 being the least strong and five being very strong), how strong are each of your feelings related to this challenge?
- How will your feelings help or hinder your actions given this challenge?
- How can you set some feelings aside to allow you to move forward with this challenge?
- Complete this sentence. If I were self-confident, I would...
- An attitude is a settled way of thinking or feeling about someone or something. What attitudes come to mind when you think about this challenge?

- On a scale of 1-5 (1 being not very and five being very committed), how dedicated are you to thinking and feeling this way?
- Is another way to think about this challenge that might make it easier to approach/cope with it?
- Complete this sentence. If I were flexible, I would...
- Given the option, would you choose to address this challenge alone or with others?
- Can you explain your choice to respond alone or with another?
- If you could choose just one person, who would you prefer to help you address this challenge and why?
- A skill is the ability to do something well. What specific skills do you have that could be used to address this challenge?
- Complete this sentence. If I were skilled in this area, I would...
- If you chose to work on this challenge with another, what specific skills does your chosen partner have that could be used to address this challenge?
- Are there skills that you and your chosen partner lack that could be helpful in addressing this challenge?
- Can you identify/connect with another who might have those skills?
- Values are the principles that help you to decide what is right and wrong, and how to act in various situations. What values/beliefs guide you as you think about this challenge?

- On a scale of 1-5 (1 being the least firm and five being very firm), how firmly do you hold these values/beliefs?
- How will these values/beliefs help or hinder your actions given this challenge?
- How can you reconcile the need to act on this challenge with your values/beliefs?

There are no right or wrong applications here. The idea is to allow participants to practice applying Skills & Attitudes that they may have never considered as an option before. Participating in group discussion moves BounceBack from a cognitive exercise to an experiential one. By encouraging participants to coach one another, the 10 Skills and Attitudes begin to drive the process. Participants are making connections/communicating. Rigid thinking is likely to be challenged, and alternatives suggested. Problem-solving and strong feeling may arise and discussed. Positive group feedback encourages self-confidence. Those who struggle with finding the purpose/meaning and seeing the big picture will have the benefit of experiencing others having more developed skills in that area. The use of appropriate humor may be a difficult concept for some. Discussion can lead to examples and a newfound appreciation of that skill. All the while, participants are not only caring for themselves and their thoughts/ideas as a group participant, they are caring for others with whom they relate by providing positive feedback. With such practice, we expect not only that the Skills & Attitudes developed will carry over into the daily challenges we all face, but participants will become a naturally active peer coach as well.

F. The Role of Artificial Intelligence and Coaching.

<u>Coaching with Technology.</u>

As we have seen in previous chapters, the process of coaching is an intrinsically human endeavor most accomplished when the coach is a good match with the issues, and a healthy relationship of trust develops. The more a person being coached feels safe to explore thoughts and feelings the more likely meaningful breakthroughs can happen which accelerate their path towards desired outcomes.

There are, however, limitations to exclusively human coaching interactions. For many people, these limitations include awareness, time, money, access, and maybe in some circumstances, stigma. As coaches ourselves, we highly value the work of our peers and embrace The International Coach Federation's (ICF) definition of coaching as; *"Partnering with clients in a thought-provoking and creative process that inspires them to maximize their personal and professional potential."* This approach is the work we all aspire to do. However, as seen below, there are limitations to remove with both coaches and people in need.

<u>Further Exploration of the Five Limitations.</u>

Awareness: Frequently people's idea of a coach is an expert in a subject and shares their expertise with another (a good example is a sports coach or nutrition coach). This type of coach, although maybe not easy to access, is well understood when an individual wants to build mastery in an area. However, what if an individual is struggling, just trying to navigate the volatile, uncertain, complex and ambiguous nature of life and work, where do they turn for help? Do they know that a coach could help them? Our definition of a coach is represented by the quote

"Coaching is unlocking a person's potential to maximize their performance. It is helping them to learn rather than teaching them." Timothy Gallwey. How aware are people of coaching in the context of improving their skills of reflection, decision making and critical thinking and the benefits these can bring?"

Time: Coaching appointments need to be scheduled, time and frequently a meeting location agreed upon (although increasingly coaching is being done via phone or skype). Appointments are planned, never spontaneous, and often end up conflicting with other obligations and commitments which complicates access.

Money: Coaching appointments generally last an hour or more and are scheduled in groups of 4–6 sessions across a period of weeks. These sessions cost from $50-$75 per hour at the low end to several hundred at the high end. The cost of coaching limits many people from accessing coaching services.

Access: How do you find a coach; how do you know how to pick a coach that is a good match for you? Are there coaches available where you live or work? How easy is it to find a coach?

Stigma: Is it OK to ask for help? Does asking for help demonstrate weakness? Should I not be able to sort all my problems myself? What will others say if I suggest I need coaching?

Many of the above limitations are removed when the human coach is not required to be present, at least not all the time. Significant advances in technology over the past few years now make it possible to consider using technology to power some types of coaching conversations which can give access to millions of people that are reached using exclusively human coaching models.

We are seeing companies, educational establishments and even cities looking at the technology of coaching to reach a much wider audience than could ever have been considered before. Bringing coaching at scale to millions of people in no way dilutes or diminishes the unquestionable value of human coaches and human interaction, but there is an access issue that technology solves and at a fraction of the cost.

About AI

PocketConfidant uses machine learning and natural language processing to build a virtual coaching technology. The technology analyzes the user input from interactions with its intelligent agent. Natural language understanding, built on sentence classification, guides the coaching conversations, while machine learning improves user engagement.

What Are We Building?

At **PocketConfidant AI**, we have coaching expertise, we are entrepreneurs, and we are building an innovative coaching conversation technology using a chatbot. A chatbot is a computer program (algorithm) that reproduces human conversation.

We don't think a chatbot "is" a coach; we believe that a chatbot "can" do the following:

- Have a coaching conversation and ask you right questions
- Facilitate a dialogue where you can become your own observer and figure things out by yourself
- Help you develop your self-coaching approach
- Build a relationship in which the conversation becomes easy for you
- Be ethical, respect your choices, remain neutral as there is no human bias possible

What Are the Goals?

It is not our goal to replace a human coach. As mentioned earlier there are limitations to the scalability of coaching if we can only have human coaches and our goal is to be able to offer coaching conversations to millions to accelerate and support awareness, reflection, and learning. There are significant advantages to using technology as a support tool for coaching;

- the bot is available 24/7 anywhere in the world on a mobile device.
- At a fraction of the cost of a human coach.
- Can partner with a human coach to support their coachee between appointments.

- Can even, as some of our coaches do, work alongside the human coach enabling the coach to take a meta position.

<u>Essential Questions to Ask and Answer</u>.

How do we work with the development of AI coaching to ensure it stays ethical?

- We're building AI with the core principles of Coaching: good listening, questioning, providing no advice and no influence; an AI that is anchored in a "mindset of neutrality" and supervised by the ethical engagement of its founders, engineers and advisory board. To develop that moral aspect, or competence, with users, we are teaching the machine to question users on the impact their decisions may have on others so that they can step back just enough to become more aware of the consequences of their actions.

- We're building an AI deliberately engaging a multi-cultural team of women and men engineers, ever vigilant to ensure that human bias won't be present to deliver a neutral, practical and active listening experience.

- Our product is built on privacy, confidentiality, anonymization and a no-sharing rule when working with clients and providing Pocket

Confidant's solution to thousands of users in the same ecosystem.

<u>Observations from Coaches on the Value of Coaching with Technology:</u>

"I help basketball high-achievers get winning results. I specialize in helping team executives, coaches, players, and entrepreneurs make a deep impact in their lives, career, team or business. I see a great opportunity to accelerate results using this technology. Typically, coaches and clients have meaningful conversations on a weekly, bi-weekly or even monthly basis. Using the PocketConfidant tool, which is available 24/7, a user can advance the "coaching conversation" without having to wait for the next phone call with their coach leading to the acceleration of more meaningful conversations when they do speak. Thus, I believe, getting to life mission clarity, goals, action plans, and results quicker and more efficiently."
- Terry Frederick, Success Coach and Strategist.[2]

An example of coach ~ technology partnership as the coach observes the coachee interfacing with PocketConfidant:
"Another complete revelation for me as a coach is also to have the time to completely immerse myself in the space of silent observation of someone completing a task and watching how they go about it. It also gives me, the coach an opportunity to think of better questions to ask as well as what feedback or closing comments may be appropriate and what may be the

---

[2] . https://www.linkedin.com/in/terry-frederick-success-coach-and-strategist-7793a6125/

best questions to identify what actions can result from the discussion. (Benefit: The opportunity to sit and observe and formulate powerful questions to ask as opposed to issues that may not be as insightful or valuable to the coachee.)"
- Richard Day PCC, "Potential," Leadership & High-Performance Coach[3]

Comments from users of our conversational technology:

"PocketConfidant is a game changer. It helps me to power up my creative problem-solving skills and enables me to overcome roadblocks at any time I choose - day or night. It's a great tool for getting me out of 'stuck' and into movement in less than thirty minutes. I can't count the number of times I've wanted to email my coach at 11 pm. The opportunity to be able to tap into empowering 'boosts' between sessions on my own is unbelievably helpful. I thrive during face to face catch-ups with my coach. So, to maintain momentum between sessions is a huge help. I'm able to arrive at my sessions with additional insights, and those insights help facilitate quicker and greater shifts. Simply stated, PocketConfidant helps me get more from my coaching. It's next level stuff."
-Matt Thomas, Coaching Client

"The process helped me hone in on the crystal core of my main insight. I completed a project within 24 hours when I had given myself five days. And, I did it with the supporting memories of the coaching as a reminder to stay on track. I have told a few people

---

3 . *https://www.facebook.com/potentialistlbli/*

about this experience. I see now how someone who thinks about going to a counselor or wanting to have a life coach but is too busy or cannot be at a certain place at a certain time, PocketConfidant is the solution."

-Dr. Leslie Gargiulo, CEO, California Intercontinental University.[4]

"I tend to avoid expressing the details about my situation, but because PocketConfidant continues to ask for more information – the who, what, when, where, how questions – it is easier to develop a better picture of the problem I have."

PocketConfidant AI

Our relationship with Dr. Ron Breazeale was inspired by reading an article in Psychology Today: "Eleven Skills and Attitudes That Can Increase Resilience." [5] We looked at how these eleven could be supported and accessed using technology.

At PocketConfidant AI we are seeking to build and increase the capacity for individuals, communities, regions, and nations to be more resilient; we envision the possibility of a better life and better world for all of us and want to make a positive and meaningful contribution. We are building an Intelligent coaching technology powered by Artificial Intelligence accessible 24/7 on any chat interface. It is designed to support individuals navigating life's challenges and transitions and is a smart app that guides the user through a questioning cycle asking the right question

---

[4] . https://www.linkedin.com/in/**leslie-gargiulo**-482a0b12
[5] . https://pocketconfidant.com/11-competencies-building-resilience-digital-world/

at the right time. It organizes user's thoughts, facilitating a stepping back from emotional challenges and allows for and promotes reflection and the formulation of a plan.

PocketConfidant is a tool, much like Dr. Breazeale's novel, that supports individuals on their life path building skills along the way to increase their capacity for reflection, learning, and resilience. It is a place where individuals can work with their stories. Our goal is to provide anyone in the world with efficient, real-time, safe and private support using "coaching as a service" in a digital technological tool. Our vision is to build an ethical and impactful solution that anyone can benefit from; which is influence-free, does not push information or solutions towards the user and does no harm.

It is not our intention to replace the human coach or trusted friend but to be present in any moment when human support cannot be there (at 2 am, or when needed at a fraction of the cost of a human coach). We have strong partnerships with coaches all over the world who use PocketConfidant as a tool to support their coachee's between sessions, or after completing a series of sessions to maintain their coaching muscle, increase resilience and sustain wellbeing.

With backgrounds in Computational Neuroscience, Education, Entrepreneurship, Education, Design, and Coaching, we are a multinational and multigenerational team driven by passion and creativity. In 2014 we were asking ourselves the question "how can we help empower people, at scale, and at a minimum cost?" Our work and development are the answer to that question. We are finding a way to scale the acquisition and delivery of essential life-skills for individuals in a personal, private and on-going way.

A couple of examples of how technology supports two of the skills of resilient people.

Skill #1:   Being Connected to Others.

Relationships that provide support and care, both within and outside the family that offer love, encouragement, and reassurance – e.g., talking with a friend. Although the importance and value of face to face and in personal relationships can never be diminished, the reality is we are living in an increasingly virtual world, where we use mobile devices as an extension of ourselves. We connect with others through Facebook, Snapchat, and other social media sites. We feel connected at 3 am when we can follow a friend's day through their posts. Something happens that sparks our thinking of someone, and while the time is not right to pick up the phone and call, we can and do, send a quick message to connect. We can agree that exclusively digital exchanges are not suitable for human well-being, but there is indeed a time and place today for conversations within these devices. Mobile devices and virtual platforms are personal, self-paced and (based on user preference) private spaces where individuals feel comfortable to open and share what's going on in their lives. It is also where they seek to support. Therefore we are reaching out to individuals on their preferred chat interfaces, in a confidential way with powerful dialogue techniques, to help them self-reflect, express their concerns and challenges, question themselves and identify solutions and or actions to move forward. Feeling empowered because of defining and creating action steps to deal with one's challenges brings increased self-confidence, and in this more open and receptive state, a desire to connect more frequently and closely with others.

Skill #2. Being Flexible.

Flexibility in thinking and actions – e.g., willingness to try something new. Mobile devices and the internet have given us perhaps the maximum flexibility we could imagine in our daily life. Ordering a pizza while in the metro, browsing a bookstore from home, making a doctor's appointment at midnight, or reaching out to family and friends while commuting would all have been impossible 20 years ago. We reach for our mobile devices for solutions to our needs of daily living all the time. In our super fast-moving world, we need to pause, reflect and find the reset button. When we become aware of a strategy not working for us, it is time to reflect on the actions we are taking, evaluate their efficacy and seek new ways of thinking. Being able to access a personal space for reflection and evaluation anywhere, at any time, on any platform, that records our thought and processing of the problem and our chosen solution, give us a way to develop improved flexibility in our thinking.

We are delighted to be partnering with Dr. Ron Breazeale and his team to bring resilience skills to an ever-expanding worldwide audience via the use of technology. We are discussing here how technology can increase access to these skills via mobile devices. We intend to open the dialogue to what advances Artificial Intelligence can bring, how it can support existing initiatives and give millions of more people access to programs of self-development.

Mission and Role.

Our mission is to create a solution for self-reflection and personal growth that empowers individuals and organizations in an ethical, flexible, scalable and inexpensive way. We are choosing to be attentive listeners, life-long learners and to pioneer capacity building through A.I.

Embrace Your Potential

CHAPTER Two
The Primary Goals of Coaching -An Overview

Coaching as it relates to work and one's personal life has three primary goals. The first is fulfillment. Fulfillment is defined by the individual that you are coaching. It is an intensely personal matter. It may involve moving up within an organization, making more money, being able to afford a new home, etc. On a deeper level, for most of us, it means feeling good about what we are doing and satisfied with our performance in the different roles that we have. If people cannot get past the idea that fulfillment involves having more "stuff," if satisfaction is seen only as an end state, and the achievement of a goal, most will be continually dissatisfied with what they have accomplished and been looking ahead rather than being focused on the present and enjoying what they have. Reaching a point where we can see fulfillment as an ongoing process is often difficult. Our work has much to do with how we feel about our lives. The more fulfilled we are with the things that we do daily, the more likely we are to be satisfied with our job and remain. A primary goal of coaching is to help the individual to feel fulfilled with their professional and personal life.

> *A primary goal of coaching is to help the individual to feel fulfilled with their professional and personal life.*

A second primary goal of coaching is to help the person being coached find balance in their life. A balanced life involves all the significant areas of a person's life including relationships with family and friends, finances, health, work, recreation, and spirit. All these pieces of a person's life are connected. Changing one impacts others. Keeping a balance often involves widening the range of options that you have and the choices that you make. Helping the individual, you are working with to say yes or no to these options can move the person toward a more balanced, and therefore a more satisfying, life. As with fulfillment, balance is not an in-state or a goal that one achieves. Life is continuously changing; consequently, one's balance in life is also evolving. Helping the individual to see whether they are moving toward or away from balance is a vital goal of the coaching process.

The third primary goal of coaching is to build resilience. For individuals to find fulfillment in their lives or to maintain balance in their lives, they must be resilient. Resilience involves the ability to bounce back, to deal with adversity well. If people are to find satisfaction in their lives, they must expect the best but prepare for the worst. The many skills involved in resilience, such as realistic planning and problem-solving, the ability to manage strong emotion and flexibility, allow the balance to be restored when it has been disrupted by a tragedy or a crisis. For all these reasons, a third primary goal of coaching is to assist individuals in building resilience.

The relationship that you are establishing with the individual that you are coaching is at the heart of the coaching process and key to its success. It is unique since it is focused on the agenda of the individual being coached. It is what they want and what they define. It must be an alliance and a partnership. When it works, it is a robust relationship both for the coach and for the person being coached? It is a place where the individual can be refocused and re-energized. It can take place over the phone, face to face, or in cyberspace with email.

As a coach, your goal is to establish a relationship based on mutual trust, confidentiality, sincere and honest information, and feedback, and a willingness to focus on all the different aspects of an individual's life; the whole person. This condition is a significant challenge. Confidentiality always has its limits. Unless you are a licensed healthcare professional or an attorney, the person you are coaching has no protection under the law regarding confidentiality. If the person that you are coaching confides in you that he is planning on breaking the law or harming himself or someone else, you may feel morally and ethically bound

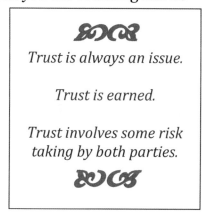

Trust is always an issue.

Trust is earned.

Trust involves some risk taking by both parties.

to break confidentiality and to inform the individual threatened or the police or to take other actions to protect the person you are coaching. You may want to discuss with the person you are working with what you see as the limits of confidentiality so that he/she understands this at the very beginning of the coaching process.

Trust is always an issue. Within large organizations, the trust of fellow employees, and especially supervisors and administrators, may not be high. If you live or work in the same community as the individual that you are coaching and have contact with his family, friends and fellow employees, the trust may be even more complicated and perhaps more challenging to create and maintain. Trust is something you must earn and usually achieve through experience with the person that you are coaching. It involves some risk-taking by both parties.

Being truthful and straightforward is sometimes difficult. It is always easier to tell the other person what you think they want to hear than what the truth may be. The person being coached may have a difficult time admitting problems or difficulties. The coach may also have trouble giving straight honest feedback. However, being straightforward and honest is an integral part of the coaching relationship that makes it work and gives it power.

Dealing with the whole person can also be a complicated process. Frequently employers attempt to define work relationships in such a way that personal issues are not brought to or addressed at work. The coaching process must treat the whole person. As we have said, all aspects of an individual are connected. A coach will not be effective if he/she encourages the person to merely put his or her personal life aside when they come to work. If they attempt to deal with only one aspect of that individual's life, without realizing that it is connected to all the other parts of their being, they will miss the whole person. Being aware of the whole person does not mean that you must deal with or fix or change all the issues or problems that the person that you are coaching may have. It does require, however, that if you are aware of these issues in the person's life, and they are not ones appropriate for you to coach the person on, you should encourage them to get whatever additional help they may require through their employee assistance program, their family physician, their priest, minister or rabbi, or a psychologist or therapist. Their health insurance in many cases will pay for these services.

Creating an alliance that involves trust, confidentiality, honesty, and a willingness to focus on all aspects of a person's life is a challenging task. The person being coached must voluntarily agree to participate in the process actively and must actively assist you, the coach, in defining and re-defining the agenda and the process of coaching. Helping the person to make this commitment and to engage in this process first, actively involves getting them to talk about the present and the future and how they would make them different. Getting the person to begin to talk about their goals and their dreams of the future, what pushes and pulls them forward, will depend upon the alliance you have with them.

In your role as the coach, you will attempt to provide them with support, feedback, and new skills that will move them toward their goals. Your focus as their coach will be on the present and the future, not on the past. This is one of the things that differentiate coaching from counseling and therapy. It is future and present focused. As part of this process, you will ask good questions that stimulate conversation and thinking and help an individual to see things from a different point of view. You may request that they take specific actions and try certain things out. A request, not a demand, and the person has the right to say no. They are, in the end, in control of this process and active participants in it.

You will also help the person to re-think failure and success. Assisting the individual to deal with both is part of the process. Encouraging them to deal with those elements of themselves that resist change and that may sabotage their goals and dreams is part of the coaching process. Whitworth and her colleagues have defined this as the "gremlin effect." They define the gremlin as the inner voice that "abhors change in the status quo." It is the part of us that fears a change of any kind and questions our ability to control it. As they point out, this part of us will always be there. We cannot eliminate it, but we can learn to manage and control it. They see a major goal of coaching "helping the client around the gremlin."

In summary, coaching involves defining an alliance and a partnership, a relationship that is dynamic and ongoing, one that requires confidentiality, truthfulness, trust, and a willingness to focus on the whole person. The direction of the process of coaching is determined by the person's agenda, their goals and their dreams of the future. It is present, and future-focused. It is not counseling or therapy and does not focus on past problems or issues. It is a dynamic and robust process that actively supports and facilitates the person's movement toward the goals that they have defined. It involves the coach providing the individual with feedback, support, and new skills. It consists of asking questions, being curious, and requesting that the person take specific actions. It is an active learning process. The primary goals are to move the individual toward a sense of fulfillment daily and assist the individual in creating and restoring balance in all areas of their lives. To be successful, the person must permit the relationship to develop and take an active role in managing and defining the process.

CHAPTER Three
Developing a Peer Coaching Program

Organizations rely on several control mechanisms to keep employees on task and minimize problems. Prominent among them are supervisors, rules and regulations, policy, and other performance measurement systems. This is standard fare and has worked quite well for decades. Some of the success emerges from employees who are not experiencing issues or needs and are mostly content in their work. We also know that negative issues occur and when they do it can negatively impact on the individual, affecting family, work, and other life engagements. Do we hope they improve, tolerate, and find them offensive; or, if within guidelines that warrant providing guidance and assistance merely be prepared to engage. Historically, organizations with peer coaching programs offer substantial benefit and collaboration with individuals helping them to return to the required "balance" in life.

Peer coaching programs evoke trust, confidentiality, professional assistance to get a person back to acceptable standards of behavior and performance. It may only provide a listening and guidance discussion, assistance in obtaining new skills and knowledge, to share information, ideas and intervene where appropriate. We are quick to say that coaching is also deemed providing necessary assistance, helping someone overcome barriers, to assist in finding a solution to pressing problems. Thus, the coach becomes a teacher, guide and source of information.

Important to coaching is the careful review of issues and finding a path forward, a plan, to overcome them. Accomplished through dialogue, assistance, and engaged problem-solving to find sustainable solutions. Peer coaching runs from formal to informal engagement, dependent on the situation and needs to be addressed. Included are several roles that may be assumed by the peer coach, and include the following:

- Mentor
- Facilitator
- Sounding board
- Provides feedback
- Helps establish new goals
- Provides problem-solving guidance
- Assists in locating resources and information
- Provides direction, information, and references
- Provides stories of other successful techniques
- Collaborates with the individual to accomplish change

Assisting in guiding ideas and strategies

A. When an employee experiences a problem at work, the presence of a peer coach can be an essential variable to satisfactory solutions. The goal is to restore balance to the employee, and the organization as harmony is important. Addressing issues is critical, as left unaddressed, tend to exacerbate. The peer coach provides personal experience, skills, knowledge, and experience that is relevant to an organization and its employees. In that role, he brings expertise and concern for the well-being of both the employee and the organization. The peer coach brings to the table qualities useful to restore balance and performance.

B. Provide feedback to the employee to questions, observations and to address outstanding issues.

C. Determine and define any problems encountered, drill down to collect information, assess that information and then determine what sustainable solutions discussed with the employee.

D. Work with the employee and the organization to review and correct wrong actions, review standards and policy, and then help determine solutions and fix the outstanding issues.

E. Determine if additional training or education is needed and assist in planning for that to happen.

F. Determine what other needs might exist including training, equipment, technology or other job-supporting information needs.

G. If a promotion or advanced job is considered, it may be fortuitous to have the peer coach assist the employee.

Peer Coach Qualifications.

1. Demonstrate a trusting relationship.
2. Demonstrate confidentiality.

3. Build personal confidence.
4. Assist employees who need guidance.
5. Improve collaboration among individuals and groups in the organization.
6. Maintain open communications.
7. Engage in organizational change where appropriate.
8. Work to overcome problems to find an appropriate solution.

A Definition of Peer Coaching[6]

Using the list from *scribd.com*, "7-Steps-to-Building-a-Coaching-Plan," the following list is provided.

1. Teach others
2. Discuss assessment data
3. Share ideas and resources
4. Guide collaborative planning
5. Expand, refine, and build new skills
6. Develop and articulate change efforts
7. Solve problems or address workplace challenges
8. Recreate informal assessments to measure employee performance
9. Implement new strategies, including the integrated use of technology

---

www.scribd.com/doc/17065092/7-Steps-to-Building-a-coachingPlan

10. Examine and study with the goal of improving practice to maximize success

In summary, they state, peer coaching can assist in reducing tension, mistakes, assisting in the implementation of new programs, promotion, and other individual and group needs. Development of a peer coaching planning process addresses four categories of the potential application allowing you to focus on the target audience. In effect, you are selecting what you want to build a plan around. Whichever one is selected there are similarities of need and program, the specifics inherent in the intended audience.

Table 1.
Categories for Planning a Peer Coaching Process

Individual	Occupational	Organization	Group/Community
A health issue, fiscal crisis, death in the family, loss of a job, poor performance.	The workplace is moving, reduction in workforce, new supervisor, need for skills upgrading	New management, new technology, transfer, product changes, location change, etc.	Environmental, pending storm, crime issue, increased danger, unplanned changes, etc.
1. Self-help 2. Bring order to chaos 3. New direction needed	1. Unit level 2. Division level 3. Retraining needed 4. New members	1. Restructuring of jobs, implications for what you do 2. New problems to be addressed	1. Volunteers 2. Fraternal 3. Committee 4. Citizens / family / groups

	to train & familiarize		

CHAPTER Four
Time and Commitment

Coaching requires a time commitment of at least a half an hour to an hour a week. It involves scheduling a regular time to talk, either over the phone, email, or face to face. And, the meeting must be in a place that affords confidentiality and free of interruptions that can inhibit this process. In addition to the time commitment of your actual session, both coach and coachee should take time to work outside of these meetings. This action will involve the individual perhaps following through with actions requested in the coaching session, trying out a different approach to a situation, or collecting additional information, etc.

Being able to plan how you devote time in the hours available and achieve the tasks you have set out, is essential to be effective. Often the available time seems too short and we attempt to cram in more than is feasible, the outcome not as we would prefer. Developing a plan for how you will use the time available, what you will include in those hours, establishing the goals to be accomplished and monitoring your time all lead to improved outcomes. Occasional adjustment is needed to address a critical incident, emergency, or another unanticipated event. Considering this helps with decision-making and overall planning when the variable of importance is involved.

A measure is how well you have successfully managed your time. Examination of your schedule demonstrates the history of engagements allowing anticipation of similar demands in the future.

Planning reduces your stress and grants you a more productive use of time. One must also consider the coachee's' need for time not engaged with others, leisure time or attention to other duties and responsibilities. Keeping a record of your planned day, what took place and where the unusual event occurred altering your plans, allows for future planning.

For the coach, this will require taking time to review the progress that has been achieved and consider the next steps in the process from the coachee's perspective. It will allow an opportunity to talk with and receive support and backup from other coaches. This extended support can be achieved through regular peer support groups for coaches, regularly scheduled each month calls and face-to-face contact between these sessions. Active coaches are supported and have a backup from their peers, and other professionals that can assist them in sorting out issues that may not be appropriate for coaching. This assistance also allows for identifying issues that require the attention of another professional (e.g., clinical psychologist, minister, or other professional).

Coaching can be done at other times and in alternative ways. It may be spontaneous assistance that you provide to a person who is working through a new problem that they confront on the job or was conveyed in a conversation with the person. It may also involve a senior employee who is guiding a new employee with job familiarization and orientation. There are many opportunities to do coaching. Some aspects of coaching are formal, setting aside a specific place and time to meet and review progress. Information coaching may also be informal; it merely occurs on the job. Being aware of these opportunities and taking advantage of them is part of being a competent coach.

Coaching others is a substantial responsibility. A person engages in coaching to build cohesiveness, to assist others in overcoming problems, and to support the individual to move forward in life, work and relationships. Some jobs are incredibly stressful where people are doing them encounter all manner of barriers that negatively impact their emotions, mental health, their family and their general health. Being able to reach out to someone and work with them is rewarding beyond the job one does and is an invaluable service to another person.

Small Group Exercise
What type of time commitment would you and your community/organization have to make, and would you be willing to make to develop and implement a coaching program?
Report Out & Discuss

CHAPTER Five
Coaching and the Change Process

Coaching is usually about change. Seldom do we coach for the maintenance of the status quo. The process of coaching, as we have defined it, is a dynamic process. It is a tool to encourage and facilitate change.

But why do people need to be coached to change? The reason, because change is difficult. Old habits and ways of doing things die hard. Anyone who has ever attempted to give up smoking understands how difficult the change process can be. If our behavior were always ruled by logic, giving up smoking would be a no-brainer. The damage smoking creates, and the benefits of stopping are well documented. But how many times have you seen people start the change process and stop? They're smoking again after a week or so.

Change is especially hard if someone is telling us we must change. For example, change in public safety organizations is often mandated. A new City Council or a new Chief may have new ideas about how to do things. Unfortunately, the officers in the field are often not ready to change. Some may have given no thought to the need for change; others may be weighing the pros, and the cons but are still not sure that what is being proposed is a good idea. Most have not decided to change. Unfortunately, the "training program" that these officers are often directed to, that is supposed to help them implement the new program or policy, may assume that they are onboard, with the change process, that they have weighed the pros and the cons and agreed with the change and that they have made a decision to go forward and that all they need are the actual steps and the tools to implement the new program. Since these assumptions are often false, the new program often fails for lack of support and commitment by administration and line officers. The bottom line: the department and the individual officers, were not ready for the change that the City Council or the new Chief tried to implement.

The Transtheoretical Model of Change

Change is stressful even if the change is "good" for you, for your family, or your community. Change requires that you think and behave differently. But most of all it requires that you are ready to change. The concept of readiness for change is not new. James Prochaska[7] and his colleagues in Rhode Island have been studying the change process for many years. They initially looked at how people change certain health habits, such as smoking. They concluded that individuals who are involved in the change process progress through a series of five stages: 1) pre-contemplation, 2) contemplation, 3) preparation and decision, 4) action and 5) maintenance.

---

7 . Prochaska, JO.; DiClemente, CC. The transtheoretical approach. In: Norcross, JC; Goldfried, MR. (eds.) Handbook of psychotherapy integration. 2nd ed. New York: Oxford University Press; 2005. p. 147–171. ISBN 0-19-516579-9.

In the first stage, <u>Pre-contemplation</u>, an individual is not thinking about making a change. They may not be

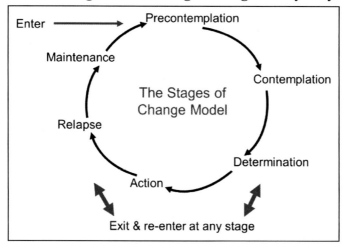

opposed to change but they may just see no need to change. If an amendment is proposed, pre-contemplates may feel that the difference is being imposed on them and may resist it. They usually do not see any significant benefits to the proposed change and may feel that the present way of doing things works or if it doesn't that there is no better alternative or option. Dr. Prochaska and his colleagues at Pro-change, an organization that focuses on helping organizations to implement new programs, estimate that in most organizations 40% of the employees may be at the pre-contemplation stage when a new program or project is proposed. They have also found when organizations actively involve pre-contemplates in the change process that the vast majority can participate in the process by sharing their concerns and can progress to the next stage, which is Contemplation.

In the second stage, <u>Contemplation</u>, the individual is taking a serious look at the pros and cons of change. They may see more clearly the benefits of change than the pre-contemplation, but they have not yet decided to change. To others, they may appear ambivalent, confused, and perhaps viewed as resistant to change. These individuals are involved in the process of weighing the pros and cons. Prochaska estimates that 40% of employees in an organization are often in the contemplation stage when the change process begins. If actively and appropriately involved, contemplators can move to the next step, referred to as the decision or preparation stage.

In the third stage, <u>Preparation & Decision</u>, a person decides to change. They are no longer ambivalent about the change process but are ready to move ahead. Prochaska estimates that 10-20% of the employees of most organizations, at the beginning of a new program, are in the preparation stage. Unfortunately, if there is considerable resistance to the change process from their colleagues who are at the pre-contemplation or contemplation stage, these individuals who are ready to move ahead with the change process may become demoralized and question whether the program or the new initiative should be implemented. If supported, however, these individuals can serve as role models to other employees.

In the fourth stage, <u>Action</u>, an individual is in the process of implementing the new changes and making the new program work. As we have said earlier, most training programs are geared to individuals either at the preparation or the action stage. The assumption is that individuals in the organizations have made a commitment to the change process and are only looking for the tools to implement the new program or policy. Unfortunately, the minority of employees in most organizations are at this stage. This is the stage where individuals need specific information and tools for implementing the new initiative or program. When individuals are forced into the action stage by their organization, the product they create is often not a very positive one. Individuals who are not adequately prepared for change tend not to do well implementing a new program. Prochaska considers this the number one reason why organizations fail at change efforts. They are asking their employees to act before they are prepared to do so. Making a change is hard enough even if one is prepared. It is difficult to implement new ways of behaving or thinking.

It's easy to return to old habits and to lapse back into the earlier stages of the change process. The fifth and last stage of change, <u>Maintenance</u>, focuses on helping individuals to maintain the changes that they have made. The focus is on supporting new patterns of behavior so that they eventually become an automatic habit.

For example, where do community policing and the coaching process fit with the model of change that has just been described? Community policing is a new way of doing business for police departments. These ways of thinking and behaving are entirely different from past models of professional policing. The skills required of the police officer are different, as well as the personality characteristics that may make for a successful community police officer. The implementation of community policing requires significant changes from all members of the department if the potential for this new way of doing business is to be actualized.

Community policing, like many new programs, has been seen by many officers as a fad. Officers, especially those in middle management and police administration who have spent most of their careers operating on the professional policing model, may not see the need to implement community policing. One would assume that many of these individuals are at the pre-contemplation stage. They are not ready to implement a new program like community policing. An equal number may be at the contemplation stage. They can see some of the pros, but they can also look at the cons. They are not committed. They have not decided.

Coaching is a tool for assisting people with the change process. Coaching focuses on where individuals are, not where we would like for them to be. It can provide a person with increased awareness and information about the benefits of change. It can also give people an opportunity to express the negative emotions that they may feel about change and can be a place for them to deal with their frustration, anger, and fear.

Coaching provides an opportunity for self and community re-evaluation

Coaching can also give the person an opportunity for self-re-evaluation to

Coaching focuses on where individuals are, not where we would like for them to be.

consider how their identity, happiness, and success could be enhanced by changing. Coaching is empowering. It can help the person see where they fit in and how they can be an essential part of their community.

The above interventions work best with individuals who are in the pre-contemplation and contemplation stage of change. Once the individual has decided to implement the change, e.g., find a new job, and has moved into the action stage, a coach can support the individual as they substitute new behaviors and ways of thinking for old ones. Coaching can also help the person find ways of rewarding themselves for their unique way of working. The coach can provide social and emotional support for the change process and can help the individual being coached re-structure their world in such a way as to make the change process more accessible to implement and to maintain.

Granted, individual and group coaching is just one tool for facilitating the change process. The community must find ways of informing its members about the benefits of the new program, e.g., methods of raising awareness of the pros and cons of changing or not changing, and ways of re-enforcing and supporting their members as they go through the change process. But coaching can be a critical part of this change process since it focuses on the individual and their agenda. The coaching process can be an invaluable tool to assist organizations/communities in implementing new programs and in providing an active process that helps individuals in dealing with all the other changes that they may desire to make or that their organization may feel that they must make. Coaching is a robust process for helping the individual and the police, and organizations and the community maintain their balance and move forward in a world that is constantly changing.

Coaching, Leadership and the Change Process: Utilizing the Processes of Change

A good leader is a good coach. A good leader effectively uses the processes of change, and in that role, he or she does the following:

a) Provides information regarding the program and the proposed change, specifically how it will affect the person.
<Consciousness Raising>.
b) Encourages Venting. Allows the ventilation of feelings about the new program and the proposed changes.
<Dramatic Relief>.
c) Supports Self-evaluation. Helps the individual to do a self-evaluation of how the program will help them achieve their goals.
<Self Re-evaluation>.
d) Encourages Support of the Organization/Community. Helps the individual understand how making the proposed changes or implementing the new program will make their organization and community better and the negative impact on them as an individual and on their community if they do not support the proposed program or proposed changes.
<Environmental Reevaluation>.
e) Facilitates Living with Change. Helps the individual believe in their ability to accept,

implement, and live with the proposed changes and the new program.
<Self-Liberation>.

f) Provides Support. Supports and encourages employees to seek and build support networks for themselves that will assist them with the change process.
<Helping Relationships>.

g) Helps Others to Think Positively. Helps people substitute positive thoughts and behaviors for negative thoughts and actions regarding the proposed change and new program (e.g., helps them reframe the proposed change).
<Counter Conditioning>.

h) Helps Others Reward Themselves. Helps people create ways to reward themselves and provide rewards to others for implementing the new program or proposed change.
<Contingency Management>.

i) Helps Others Avoid Negativity. Helps the person avoid, deal with and manage people, places and things that attempt to put down rather than support/facilitate the change process or the new program. **<Stimulates Control>.**

j) Helps Others See the Big Picture. Helps the individual to take a broader view of the world. They support the person to see where the new changes and the new program fit into the larger scheme of things.
<Social Liberation>.

All the above processes fit within the scope of coaching and the role of the leader as coach.

Small Group Exercise
Apply the processes of change to your supervision of a specific employee. What is the behavior/attitude change you want to move the employee toward? What stage of change is your supervisee in? What processes of change will you apply? How will you do this?
Report Out & Discuss

CHAPTER Six
Goal Setting: Establishing a Path Forward.

If you are coaching someone, then you are working with them through a process that encourages them to move toward specific goals. The coaching process, therefore, involves goal setting. A goal can be specific such as passing an exam, or general, such as getting along with the new shift supervisor. The best goals are often SMART goals. This acronym refers to goals that are:

Figure 1.
S.M.A.R.T. Goals

1. Specific.
2. Measurable.
3. Attainable.
4. Realistic.
5. Time-oriented.

In other words, you know specifically what you are doing or trying to attain, you can Measure your progress toward the goal, you know that the goal is Attainable, you can reach that goal and Realistic, you can reach the goal in a reasonable amount of time with a reasonable expenditure of effort and resource, and you have set a Specific Timeframe for attaining the goal. Many people work very well with this type of structure. The process encourages accountability and requires that people move from vague and non-specific to the detailed steps that they will take in moving toward their goals.

Some people do not operate well with this approach. They find it too structured and confining. General questions about how things are going with a specific project or how close they feel they are to achieving their goal may be enough. Being okay with vague and non-specific goals and agreements may be more difficult for the coach than for the person coached. Our value and worth as a coach should not always be measured by a specific accomplishment of the person that we are coaching. Remember again, as a coach you are working with their agenda, not yours, with their goals, not with yours.

Small Group Exercise
(a) Apply SMART goal setting to a person you are "assisting" in setting up a "Readiness Kit." (b) Apply SMART goal setting to yourself.
Report Out & Discuss

CHAPTER Seven
The Difference Between Coaching, Psychotherapy, and Counseling.

Psychotherapy focuses on emotional or behavioral problems that need "therapy," that need to be healed or cured. The focus is therefore frequently on pathology and what is wrong rather than what is right. A diagnosis is usually developed, and a plan of treatment prescribed.

Professional coaching, on the other hand, focuses on what is right with the person. It focuses on their strengths and abilities and how the coaching process can facilitate the growth and development of the client and the movement of the client toward balance in their life. The client is assumed to be resourceful and creative. The whole person is addressed, not just the problem. The relationship is one of the equals. The coaching plan or agenda comes from the client, not from the coach. Coaching is focused on the positive, on learning new ways of dealing with issues and problems and on acting. The goals of coaching usually include areas of fulfillment which do not necessarily mean increasing the amount of money the client generates each year or the material possessions they own. It does mean helping the client to develop a sense of fulfillment in their heart and their soul. It focuses on being able to create a balanced life, an increased level of satisfaction in the areas of relationships, spirituality, health, and career.

Coaching, like psychotherapy or counseling, is a process. It takes time, and like psychotherapy, it involves some of the same skills. Good coaches and good therapists listen well. They can hear the client on some different levels and do not allow their issues or problems to interfere or to distort the communication process. Coaches are naturally curious like most psychotherapist and ask right questions. The focus, like Carl Rogers client-centered counseling, is on the individual being coached. Coaches, like therapists, attempt to pull together the information that they receive from the client and may state that to the client as a hunch, intuition, or gut feeling, or in the case of the therapist, their opinion. For me, one of the best things about professional coaching is that it is free of the medical model. Its focus is on self-actualization, e.g., living up to one's potential. This model, I believe, fits well with the Independent Living Movement and with the training of individuals with disabilities to serve as coaches with other individuals with disabilities.

A few other distinctions between the two, professional coaching is frequently done over the phone and now over the Internet. It does not require face-to-face contact. Because it is not a medically necessary service, it is not reimbursed under any insurance plan.

Coaching vs. Therapy[8]

Noomii, The Professional Coach Directory, provides a comparison between coaching and therapy, a concept definition that is of value to understand. Quoting from that Internet page, they made the following analogy.

> "A common misconception is that coaching is the same as therapy, when in fact they are quite different. Therapy is intended to help people recover from emotional or other psychological disorders such as depression or anxiety. Coaching, on the other hand, is intended to help normal, healthy individuals achieve personal goals such as increased happiness, weight loss, improved work-life balance. etc."

Figure 1.
A Comparison of Ten Coaching vs. Therapy

Coaching	Therapy
1. The client is emotionally and psychologically healthy.	1. The client is emotionally unwell and in need of healing.
2. Focuses on the present and the future.	2. Focuses on dealing with the past.
3. Driven by goals and taking action.	3. Driven by unresolved issues and emotional healing.

---

[8] . https://www.noomii.com/article/coaching-vs-therapy

4. Works toward a higher level of functioning.	4. Works to achieve understanding and emotional healing.
5. Results-based and focuses on exploring solutions.	5. Explores the root of problems and explains.
6. Asks, "Where would you like to be and how can you get there?"	6. Asks, "How did that make you feel?"
7. Acts on the information.	7. Absorbs information.
8. Done over the phone, internet or in person.	8. Done in an office setting.
9. Coach and client collaborate on solutions.	9. The therapist is the 'expert.'
10. Contact between sessions expected (accountability and wins).	10. Contact between sessions for crisis and difficulties only.

Above all, we want to see organizations provide a level of service to employees to assist with issues and problem-solving. The peer coach has an important role with fellow employees, to assist in the knowledge of the job, of experience and the organization's culture and policy. If the issue or problem extends beyond the peer coach's authority to engage, or when the additional depth of assistance is warranted; they should refer the individual to another process where appropriateness is found.

CHAPTER Eight
Basic Coaching Skills

To be an active listener, you must pay attention and communicate to the speaker that you are attentive. Effective listening is an active process, not a passive one. Asking good questions, paraphrasing, reflecting, etc., are all active listening skills and necessary to the coaching process.

As the authors of Co-Active Coaching point out, we can listen to different levels. We may be listening to the words of the other person to determine how what they say will impact us or what it means to us. The focus is on us. Whitworth and her colleagues point out that one way of recognizing that we are listening at this level is a desire on our part for more information. We may want answers or details. When someone is being coached, they usually are operating at Level 1. They are listening to you, the coach, regarding how what you will say will impact them and be useful to them in dealing with the challenges that they are confronting.

In Level 2, listening, the focus is more on the other person. You are focused on their tone of voice, and on the feelings that the other person is expressing. You reflect those back. Whitworth and her colleagues believe that most coaching goes on at level 2.

Level 3 listening is labeled global listening by the authors of Co-Active Coaching. Level 3 listening incorporates level 2 but is broader. At level 3 the coach is much more in tune with the person that they are coaching. They make greater use of their intuition. The ability to empathize and feel what they

are feeling is strong. They sense subtle changes in
their mood and their energy level that they might not
have noticed at level 2. To quote the authors of <u>Co-
Active Coaching</u>, "Everything in coaching hinges on
listening, especially listening with the client's agenda
in mind."

1. <u>Summarizing and Clarifying</u>

As a coach you want to help the person see clearly
what they have accomplished and what they need to
do, specifically to continue to build their resilience
and reach their goals. These two skills are helpful in
this process. The first involves giving a summary of
what has been said and agreed to. This also includes
being clear about details and specifics. It may include
writing things down so that both you and the person
that you are coaching can see what has been said and
what has been decided. Seeing things in black and
white is often helpful in the coaching process.

Clarifying is the process of moving from a vague and
general statement to a more specific and detailed one.
It often involves helping the person complete their
thoughts or be more specific or stop rambling.

Both <u>summarizing</u> and <u>clarifying</u> often lead to a
statement by you as the coach, of how what they are
saying or what has been agreed to fits into the bigger
picture. How does this relate to their goals, to their
vision, and their future? How does this move them
forward? Stating your perception of this is helpful. It
gives the individual something to bounce off and react
to and an opportunity to correct or to agree with and
expand on the picture you have painted.

If you are using this guide as part of a workshop/conference, choose someone to work with you as a training partner. If you are doing this at home, choose a friend or family member.

> **Clarifying issues and needs is critical to avoid misconceptions and filling in the blanks with guessing.**
>
> **Clarity leads to more sustainable solutions.**

Dyad Exercise I
Choice of topic. Talk with your partner about it. Practice the skill. Reverse roles. Give feedback on performance. (20 minutes – 10/10 each)
Report Out & Discuss

2. Using Your Intuition and Providing Feedback

Coaching is an active process. As a coach, you are continually providing feedback to the person that you are coaching. The feedback may be supportive, such as "you did a great job on that" or it may be critical but constructive such as "based on what you have achieved in the past I think you could have done a better job on this project. What do you think?" Feedback is always honest. Again, you are a coach, not a cheerleader.

Coaching may be confrontive. If you feel someone is avoiding an issue that they should address, you may want to call them on it. You may "know" that the problem needs to be addressed because you know the person. You have a sense of who they are, and as a coach, you may be able to see the forest and not just the trees.

Your feedback, at times, may be based on <u>intuition</u> about what will work for them. Intuition is our interpretation of what we know about the person. It is part of what we know based on our experience with the person we are working with and our experience with people in similar situations. It is our opinion. And that's all it is. We must be willing to allow the person to question or dispute it or to ignore it. It's not necessarily right. We may have logical reasons for feeling this way, but part of it is just our feelings about what will work, what is right, what is going to happen. We can't always defend it based on logic, experience, or evidence at hand.

As a coach, it is our responsibility to provide this feedback to the person. When presented it needs to be stated as our opinion or our intuition, not as "the word of God" or "the only way to do things," for we are wanting the individual we are talking with to make informed choices.

Dyad Exercise II
Talk to your partner about how you handled a situation or problem. Let them practice giving you feedback. Reverse roles. Give feedback on performance. (20 minutes 10/10 each). (20 minutes – 10/10 each).
Report Out & Discuss

3. <u>Asking Good Questions</u>

Coaches are curious by nature. They do not jump to conclusions. They ask the right questions, often known as open-ended questions, to encourage the person that they are coaching to talk more about the issue or the topic at hand. The approach has often been referred to as Socratic, referring to Socrates, who taught his students by asking questions.

Strong open-ended questions usually begin with the word how or what. They are powerful and encourage the person to talk more about a specific issue. They stop the person and require them to think. Why questions are often considered not to be good open-ended questions since they may encourage the person to explain or to justify what they have done or what they are going to do or to defend their actions. As a coach, you do not wish to encourage defensiveness.

Some of the best questions are the shortest and the simplest. On the face, they may appear naïve or "dumb." The authors of Co-Active Coaching present a list of eight "dumb" but powerful questions and include such issues as what did you learn? Where do you want to go from here? What do you want?

Playing dumb can be a way of diffusing someone who is angry by encouraging them to explain to you what is happening. It can also be a very effective way of supporting the person you are coaching to describe, interpret, and to think.

Remember; don't ask for details unless you need them. Questions that ask for specific information usually are not open-ended and often do not encourage the client to think. Yes and no questions are also considered to be closed-end questions since to answer them little work is required by the person. Yes and no questions are best used when you are working on making an agreement or a commitment. A firm yes or no is important in these situations.

Dyad Exercise III
Choice of topic. Talk with your partner about it. Practice the skill. Reverse roles. Give feedback on performance. (20 minutes – 10/10 each).
Report Out & Discuss

4. Accountability

For the coaching process to be effective, it requires accountability. You are accountable to the person you are coaching for your actions, and they are responsible for you on the issues and the agenda that you and they are addressing.

In a previous section where we discussed goal setting, we talked in some detail about accountability. The acronym SMART is used to refer to agreements or goals that are Specific, Measurable, Attainable, Realistic, and Time-oriented. As we have said previously, as a coach, you encourage the person to use these standards when setting agreements and targeting goals. You may also wish to encourage them to set up rewards and consequences to help with follow through. Part of promoting the person to move ahead may be setting up a program whereby they reward themselves for follow through and for accomplishment. The rewards may be monetary, but they may also be other tangible or non-tangible consequences, such as giving themselves more free time, vacation, etc.

You may also wish to request that the person try something or take some form of action which they may be hesitant to do. We are not referring to a direct order, but a suggestion. It remains the person's choice. You are asking. The person can either agree or disagree or a compromise between what you are offering, and they are suggesting may be shaped. The person frequently may feel that what you are asking is too much. Your role as a coach is often to challenge the person. To get them to look beyond what they think they can do and perhaps set the bar at a higher level.

To achieve their goals, the person may frequently have to make use of schedules and routines. This may be something that you wish to encourage. Asking them to make a list each morning or evening and to check off those things completed, and then to add to the agenda for the next day those things not finished. Encouraging them to prioritize what is essential and what isn't required is necessary if this form of structure is to be useful.

Accountability and structure are important and central to the coaching process. However, sometimes they may be over-emphasized and over-used. The person may be one of those people who can achieve their goals without having to get things too tied down or specific. If they can work effectively without a lot of structure, it is a good outcome. If this doesn't work and he/she fails to move ahead, using structure and accountability on a more specific and less vague basis may be required.

Dyad Exercise IV
Help your partner develop a SMART plan about a specific issue or problem. Reverse roles and give feedback on performance by the other. (20 minutes 10/10 each)
Report Out & Discuss

CHAPTER Nine
Communicating Effectively

Effective communication is key to building resilience and maintaining balance in your life. Communication is the foundation upon which we build our lives. It is the way in which we understand others and the way in which we attempt to get other people to understand and know us. If we do not communicate clearly and directly with others, we will not understand, and we will not be understood.

Many of the situations that we deal with daily are complicated. Very few are black and white. The other person usually has their side of things, their story, and their way of looking at things. If we don't take time to understand what they are saying or how they see things, we usually are not going to be very effective in dealing with them or with any problems that arise in our relationships with them. There are very few pat solutions that one can directly apply to a problem. We need to understand what we are confronting, and the only way that we are going to do that is by effectively communicating with those around us.

Many of the skills that are presented below are ones that you make use of each day in your work and personal life. They are basic "interviewing" skills. Unfortunately, many of us put these skills away when we leave work and do not apply them to the world outside of work. We may not listen well. We may be tired of listening. We have been listening to people all day. When we are tired or angry and upset, it is difficult to do this. It is especially difficult to listen to someone with whom we are angry. But if we are going to find a solution to the problems that we are dealing with, either at work or at home, we must talk, and we must listen to find out what is happening.

1. Encouraging People to Talk: Basic Communication Skills

If people are to talk with you and share information, especially if they are to say things that may be difficult to tell, they need to know that they are connecting with you. They need encouragement! If you meet their attempts to communicate with silence, or if you assume the attitude of an interrogator, you will not put other people at ease, and you will not encourage them to tell you what you need to know.

To be useful in understanding another's perspective, you need to do things which show interest and genuine concern. Here are some examples you can use to encourage other people to talk, especially in a crisis when people are upset and angry:

a) Use neutral expressions such as "I see," "Go on," "I understand," "Yes."

Acknowledging that you hear the other person, encourages them to discuss further. Spoken softly and without the intent of disrupting the other person talking, it encourages continued reflection and sharing.

2) Nod your head or smile.

Providing simple gestures demonstrates that you are engaged, listening, and paying attention to the other person speaking. Distractions tend to interrupt the discussion, and it certainly can cause someone to lose concentration and focus of thoughts. Being attentive and showing you care, is healing.

3) Try "echoing" or slightly rephrasing what the person has said.

For example: You are talking with your best friend about his wife, and he says, "I feel she's changed a lot!" You might say, "Changed?" It is very important to avoid trying to advise people at this point. Your advice is not going to be very good since you don't understand what is going on. Avoid being the cross-examiner or the fault finder or focusing on trivialities. Keep the conversation focused on present issues, the things that can be resolved. Unfortunately, as you will see in the next chapter, people often have a tough time fighting fairly and sticking with the central issues. People love to digress into trivialities and play one-upmanship games.

4) Ask good questions.

Unfortunately, people often don't know how to ask the right questions. When we're talking with someone, we need to ask open-ended questions that encourage them to talk, for example: "What happened?" or " What are you going to do now?" We often ask questions that have a "yes" or "no" answer that does not encourage discussion, or we ask people "Why" questions that often shut down discussion. Unfortunately, when we ask "why" questions we are often encouraging people to become defensive and to try to come up with some reason to justify their behavior. The reality may be that they don't know why. We could spend the rest of the evening talking about "why" when "why" really isn't that important and is not going to lead us to a solution to the problem.

5) Get down to the details.

If you are trying to find out what is happening, be specific. One of the major blocks to communicating in a crisis is the inability of people to describe what was said or done by another person. Being able to accurately describe what happened is often essential to be able to understand a very tense and complicated situation.

Being a good listener requires that you focus on observable actions of others without making value judgments or interpretations of what they meant. As a society, we love to talk in generalities. We often accuse people of behaving in a certain way because of a motive or a value that we believe is hidden behind their behavior. It can be essential to look at people's motives but at this point in the process that is not your goal. Your goal is to try to understand what is happening and what people did and said. A frequent mistake made in dealing with a crisis is our tendency to react to the accusations or generalizations that others may make or to the interpretations that others may add to another person's behavior and not to the facts, i.e., the clear, observable actions of others.

But what about the situation where you are trying to help someone through a difficult time, and you really don't care about the specifics? You simply want to be a good listener to help the person "talk it out." You're interested in helping them to understand how they're feeling and what they can do to deal with the crisis. Here are some things you can do to be a good listener.

> ## Encouraging People to Talk
>
> 1. Use neutral expressions.
> 2. Nod your head and smile.
> 3. Rephrase.
> 4. Ask good questions.
> 5. Get to details.

1) Reflect what they are saying.

This is a technique frequently used by counselors. It's a way of helping people hear themselves and understand what they are saying. Very often people need to say things out loud, and they need to hear other people's reactions to find their way.

When you reflect what a person is saying, you are not merely trying to say the same thing with different words. It is not a slick use of language that you are trying to achieve. You say back to the person what his/her statement meant to you. This gives the person you are talking with an opportunity to hear your impressions of what they are saying and to correct you if the opinion that they are providing is not accurate. It is also another way of letting people know that you care about what they are saying and that they matter to you.

Your friend may make a general statement that you respond to with a specific comment. For example, she may say "My supervisor doesn't like anything that I do at work." And you may respond by saying, "She

doesn't even like the way you make coffee?"
Sometimes your specific statements may be humorous and may encourage your friend to look more realistically at the situation that she is dealing with at work.

The reverse may also be true. Your friend may list the things that she hates about work, and you may respond by making a general statement like, "It sounds like there's nothing at your work that you like".

What your friend is saying may also recall an example that you think reflects what she is talking about. For example, your friend is saying that she feels she is being mistreated at work. You recall that she was questioned after taking a sick day and asked to bring a doctor's excuse. You may want to mention this example.

2) Another way of helping someone to get things out and talk is to use a technique called "Checking it Out."

This technique involves describing what you perceive the other person's feelings to be. By doing this, you are telling the other person that what they feel is important and you are asking the other person to say to you if you understand them. The way to use this technique is to describe the other person's feelings as accurately as you feel you can. You must do this without making value judgments. It is not helpful to tell a person that they should not feel the way they feel. Leave value judgments until later and give them only if they ask for them.

Unfortunately, past experiences and personal issues often get in the way of listening. Sometimes it is important that you invite the other person to tell you whether your description of their feelings is accurate or not. If they tell you that it is inaccurate, try to accept this. It is not a good idea to pretend that you are a mind reader and that you "really know how they feel." You may not, and by saying that you do, you are not helpful to the other person. If they are to understand their feelings, the opportunity to accept value judgments about what they should or should not be experiencing are needed.

3) And finally, a very useful technique that most of us do not practice very well in a tense situation. The method is "silence."

As the word implies, it means saying nothing. It is not a technique that tends to relax other people or that is especially relaxing for us to use when we're feeling anxious. Many of us like to talk when we're feeling tense. Silence requires that we say nothing, verbally or non-verbally.

Being silent is not a good idea for a situation that can turn violent or for a situation in which the person you are dealing with is angry with you. It tends to make other people more uptight and more anxious because it places the burden of talking on them and removes it from you.

Silence is an excellent approach to use with people to encourage them to talk more when your verbal attempts are not working. When used skillfully, silence can convey concern and interest on your part. It can encourage the silent person you're talking with to talk, to go beyond yes or no answers, and it can also keep you from having to take sides in a conflict. For example, if two friends are having an argument and want you to give your opinion as to who is correct, silence may be an excellent response.

CHAPTER Ten
Additional Coaching Skills

Strategies to Assist in the Coaching Process.

> 1. Get to the point.
> 2. Stand up for the person.
> 3. Encourage ventilation and
>   refocusing.
> 4. Reframe.
> 5. Break through old patterns of
>   thinking.
> 6. Deal with failure

Explained:

1. Get to the Point.

WHAT? Getting to the point involves focusing the person. What is the person saying? What is the question or the conclusion? Bottom line?

WHEN? When the person is rambling, and there is no time for a detailed story. When getting to the bottom line is most important.

HOW? Getting to the point involves focusing on the essential part of the conversation. What's the point he's trying to make? What does it all boil down to? What's the bottom line?

Role Play 1
<u>Medications</u> You are assisting a person with multiple physical problems in putting together an emergency kit. You are helping her to list the medications that she is taking and the size and frequency of each medication dose. The person is rambling, and you have limited time to complete the list with her since there are other appointments you have, and it will be weeks before you can reconnect with this person and the family. The person you are helping is elderly and does not like being rushed. She has some difficulty hearing and perhaps understanding what you are asking. What would you do?

2. <u>Standing Up for the Person</u>.

WHAT? Stand up for the person when he/she is unable to stand up for himself. Frequently the person you are coaching may not be able to see their abilities or accomplishments. Standing up for the person means pointing out the positive things that she may be unable to see because of her focus on her limitations and her self-critical attitude

WHEN? Apply this skill in situations where the individual is not realistically looking at themselves or when they are not accurately assessing their abilities or skills.

HOW? Standing up for and championing the person involves pointing out their skills, abilities, and strengths when they are unable to see them. This is done in a matter of fact and balanced way. This is not cheerleading! It does not involve denying weakness or problems but balances those with the person's abilities and strengths. It may include reminding them of past accomplishments or situations that they have handled successfully. You are championing the truth.

Role Play 2
Overcoming Self Doubt You are assisting an individual with multiple health problems to develop a plan for his evacuation. To survive daily, he requires a variety of medications and medical equipment that would be difficult to transport. He appears overwhelmed by the prospect of having to evacuate and leave his home. As you talk with him, he becomes more fatalistic and seems resigned to having to stay in the house even if remaining there would most likely result in his death. What would you say and do?

3. Ventilation and Re-Focusing.

WHAT? Ventilation and Re-focusing have been referred to as clearing by some authors. This allows the person to vent feelings of anger and frustration or to express self-doubts in a safe setting where they will not be judged or criticized. The goal is to allow the person to discharge and vent emotions that may be clouding their thinking and interfering with the ability to think clearly and rationally. They can then re-focus.

WHEN? Use this strategy when the individual appears to be having difficulty getting over or around an event or situation that has stirred up intense emotion such as when they are angry, embarrassed, frustrated, etc. When a crisis/tragedy has disrupted and changed their lives. When they must do something, they do not want to do, e.g., evacuate, move to a shelter.

HOW? Allow the person to vent or discharge their feelings by encouraging them to talk about what has occurred, giving them permission and support for the expression of strong emotion and passion. Allow the coachee to openly vent feelings of frustration and anger and to share angry fantasies that they may have or feelings that may be irrational. The individual does not have to be fair, rational, or just. They need to be honest and are encouraged to vent their feelings to clear these thoughts from their head. This process of ventilation will allow them to move ahead. Now refocus the person! What needs to be addressed now?

Role Play 3
<u>Controlling Temper</u> You are working with a young man who has recently been discharged from the Veterans Administration Hospital. He is an Iraqi veteran and has returned home after losing both legs and one arm. When you started talking with him about developing an emergency plan, he laughs. When you press on, and he understands you are serious, he becomes irritated and angry. He begins to attack you verbally. He is saying you have no understanding of the problems that he has been dealing with since he returned home and that developing an emergency plan is the last thing on his mind. What would you do and say?

4. Re-Framing.

WHAT? Re-framing involves getting the person to look at a situation from a different perspective. The perspective may be a new one for the individual you are coaching. It may also be more positive than the attitude from which they are viewing the experience or the situation. Re-framing is not just looking on the bright side of things. It is not empty cheerleading. It involves seeing how an unexpected turn of events may still move the person toward their goal.

WHEN? Re-framing is to be used when you believe the individual does not see the forest for the trees. When the person sees only one perspective, perhaps looking at just the negative impact of the events or the experience is too limiting and creates a barrier.

HOW? Re-framing requires that the coach be able to step back from the situation enough to look at it from a different perspective and not to become so caught up in the person's perception of a situation that he/she is unable to look at things differently. You can be empathetic and validate their perspective while adding a different angle or twist to the situation — something they have not seen. Re-framing does not involve putting on rose colored glasses or blinders. If the events are going to have a negative impact on the person, acknowledge this. You can still look for the silver lining. The lining may not be silver, but if it is different and is a new way of looking at the situation that moves them toward their goals, you have re-framed the situation. You have given them a fresh perspective.

Role Play 4
<u>Divorce</u> Tom and Susan, two close friends of yours, have recently separated. You are curious about what is happening. You call Tom and suggest that the two of you have dinner together. At dinner, Tom confides in you that he is planning on divorcing Susan because he has found out that she is involved with another man. Tom and Susan have been married now for ten years and have two children. Tom tells you that when he confronted Susan about the other relationship, she admitted that she was involved in the relationship and that she had no intention of breaking it off. Tom says he sees no other alternative but to proceed with the divorce. What would you say and do?

5. <u>Break Through Old Patterns of Thinking</u>.

WHAT? All of us carry around assumptions about how things are and will be. One of the most useful things you can do as a coach is to help people break out of old patterns of thinking, especially if they limit the person and prevent them from moving ahead. This involves getting the individual to question old assumptions and expectations, e.g., permanence, pervasiveness, personal blame.

WHEN? The opportunity to get the person to question and dispute old ways of thinking usually occurs when the person is stuck. When the individual is giving up and unable to move ahead because of their negative perspective or their assumption that the problem is unsolvable, the barrier cannot be removed, or the situation changed.

HOW? The tool for breaking old patterns of thinking is known as <u>self-disputation</u>. This involves teaching the person to question old assumptions, expectations, and perspectives of a situation or an experience. Good questions are: Does this way of thinking about the situation move me forward or cause me to give up? How do I know that what I'm expecting to happen is likely to occur? How many times have things worked out that way in the past? How do I know what I think I know? What would happen if I approached this situation with a different set of expectations, perhaps the opposite of what I'm presently anticipating? Breaking old patterns of thinking involves confrontation at times. Questioning challenges the person's way of looking at the situation, their expectations and their assumptions about how it will work and of what they and others are capable of.

Role Play 5
<u>The Merger</u> Jim's company has been recently purchased by another company. The merger resulted in Jim taking a pay cut and losing some of his benefits packages. He appeared to accept some of these changes, at least initially, saying that he believed in the company and wanted to stay with it. However, recently the company that acquired his has implemented new policies and procedures that Jim feels do not support the importance of providing responsive and quality service to clients. Jim wants

> to talk to you about his options. What would you say and do?

6. <u>Dealing with Failure</u>.

WHAT? Helping a person learn from failure and deal with it realistically and straightforward.

WHEN? When the person has failed or perceives that they have failed in achieving their goal or following through with a commitment that they have made.

HOW? Most of us carry considerable baggage around about failure. Many want to deny it and pretend it hasn't happened. Others have been taught to take a somewhat Pollyanna view and to reinterpret it in such a positive way that it is no longer perceived as a failure. Helping the person deal with failure involves dealing realistically with what has occurred and with the responsibility the individual may bear in the situation or events that you are discussing. It may include re-framing the failure as a learning experience or an opportunity. Again, it is a realistic re-framing of the situation that to work must move the person closer to their goals. This re-framing may help the individual feel better, but this is not the primary goal. Your primary goal is to help the person to learn what they need to do to move toward their goals. Analyzing what went wrong can be helpful in developing a new plan or re-directing one's efforts. Failure can be a valuable experience. It gets their attention. It brings up old assumptions and expectations that may need to be disputed so that the individual can move on.

Role Play 6

Losing Your Job

Mary has worked at the same company for the last 25 years. She has been a loyal employee and has always received excellent reviews from her supervisors. Approximately six years ago, the woman that she had been working for the last ten years retired. Mary was passed over for promotion into her boss's position, and a man younger than Mary from outside of her department was given the job. Mary has not gotten along well with her new supervisor. Three months ago, she received her first negative evaluation with a request from her supervisor for corrective action in some areas. Mary has confided in you over the last few months that she is making every effort she can to adapt to and accommodate her new boss. On Friday morning, she was called into her supervisor's office and terminated and given an hour to clear out her desk and leave the facility. She was escorted out of the building by a security guard. What do you say and do to help Mary deal with what has just happened?

CHAPTER Eleven
Coaching Resilience for Individual & Organizational Change

Coaching implies that the person coached is attempting to attain a goal or to maintain their performance. The person coached is moving, they are performing, and they are in a constant process of change. As we have discussed in the previous section, coaching can be a tool in helping an individual ready themselves for change, decide to change, and carry through and maintain changes that they have made. Coaching is a process, a relationship that is dynamic and ongoing. It is a dynamic and powerful process that actively supports and facilitates the person's movement toward the goals that they have defined. When effective it can help the person become more resilient and increase balance in all areas of their lives. Change is a constant and therefore a constant in the coaching process.

Supervisory Coaching[9].

The purpose of supervisory coaching is to guide employees to enable the fulfillment of their job responsibilities. Collectively, the achievement of job responsibilities leads to accomplishing organizational goals and mission. Employees have different sets of skills, knowledge, and experience to apply to their positions that must be harnessed to pull the wagon in

---

[9]. The following is from: Lumb, R., & Breazeale, R. (2011). Addressing Correctional Employee Behavior: The Importance of Attitude and Personality and the Role of Coaching in Facilitating Change. The Correctional Trainer, feature article, March/April, 2011, pp. 5-15

the same direction. We also know that employee attitudes and level of motivation impact their performance.

The skilled supervisor realizes that it is the people of the organization who ultimately determine its success. Knowing when an employee has the skills and motivation to perform autonomously or when an employee needs a specific direction, and close monitoring creates a continuum of supervisory interactions. Quoting Senge (1990:19), "When we focus only on our position, we do not see how our actions extend beyond the boundary of that position." In some instances, the "self-identity" becomes the driving force behind the behavior and performance creating some disconnect. A focus on our position or those close to us without a big picture view inhibits contribution and alliances within the organization that helps meet the mission and goals – the purpose of the organization's existence.

The importance of individualizing supervision to match the skill and incentive levels of each employee can be realized using clinical supervision principles and motivation theory. There are twenty-six theories of motivation, and while all offer an aspect of individual and organizational reference, we are preferential to Prochaska's "Transtheoretical Model of Change" that addresses the steps of change and maintaining personal attention to one's duties and responsibilities.

At one end of the supervision, the continuum is supervisor-controlled interaction. In the center of the continuum is a collaborative approach where the employee and supervisor share the role of establishing goals, priorities, timelines, and measures of success.

At the end of the continuum, the knowledgeable and motivated employee is more autonomous in creating the goals and measures of success (Figure 2). Knowing that opportunity for growth and advancement, recognition, challenging and stimulating work, and personal achievement are essential motivating factors, the active supervisor blends the focus of meeting organizational goals with individual goals in motivating involvement. High performance comes from the simultaneous achievement of organizational and personal goals.

Figure 2
Supervision Continuum

Supervisor Controlled →

Collaboration →

Employee Autonomy

Critical Points to Supervisor Coaching Effectiveness

- Emphasize coaching people. Help bring about change in an individual's performance and behavior by engaging with them and assisting in bringing value.

- Encourage employees to learn skills and acquire information that applies to their job. The application of these skills and knowledge is generally left to the individual to refer to his or her career and without engagement by supervisor habits, preferences, and other limiting influences reduce growth and innovation. A motivating supervisor helps the employee connect with job requirements and the broader organizational mission.

- The traditional supervisor utilizes policy, discipline, and rules to manage people under his or her direction. The goal of effective supervisor coaching is to create motivation, provide guidance and maintain accountability of the employee.

- Knowing the employee's strengths, weaknesses, goals, values, and vision allows the supervisor to move the employee toward the organization's mission and goal achievement and significant personal growth.

- Supervisors often spend too much time dealing with "nitty-gritty" details that others do not handle appropriately. This narrow attention is time-consuming and diminishes from engaging in higher order tasks.

- Supervisors must treat each employee as an individual and develop a team spirit.

- Supervisors must maintain an emphasis on the organization's mission, goals, and values.

- As a supervisor, you are accountable to the organization and the employees under your command. This is a demanding responsibility.

- Supervisors must take a systematic approach to manage people. All aspects of the work must be maintained, and employee contribution and needs are part of that emphasis.

- It is important to realize that you are not alone in the supervisor boat. Engaging with your peers and seeking their guidance and advice is healthy. The goal is to do your best in helping individuals under your supervision to become exemplary employees.

- It is imperative that supervisors continually address how the work of the department is being handled and if the work is being done effectively and efficiently.

The Role of the Supervisor as a Coach.

Supervisor coaching is designed to focus on providing individual employees with the information and skills needed to maintain balance with their job, family, friends, community and themselves. For purposes of this discussion, supervisors represent any individual who has oversight and guidance of others in the organization. Supervisor coaching focuses on skills that employees already possess and examines how they are applied to multiple situations and environments. Emphasis is on the employees' role as a problem solver. As a supervisor, you can assist individuals in developing styles of leadership and authority

Provide employees with information and skills to maintain balance with work, family, friends, and community

that are participative and authoritative rather than authoritarian.

Summary

To summarize the main ideas of this section: being resilient and maintaining balance in your life requires effective communication. Situations are complex. To understand, and to be understood, requires communication. If you are to understand, you must stop, look, and listen to your environment and adjust as needed. This may be more difficult when you are tired, angry, or upset. Practical solutions to work or family problems require effective communication. The approaches that we have outlined in this chapter give you the tools to do this. Listening and communicating are skills that can be learned, like reading. Unfortunately, many of us have not had good models in our lives for learning to communicate with others. We have often been taught ways that don't work. Very few of us have been shown how to be good listeners. But old dogs can learn new tricks.

Being an active listener is one of those new tricks we all can learn and apply.

Developing a Peer Coaching Plan

A.   A peer coach represents an essential contributor to people and groups who experience a disruption in their lives. When the challenge becomes of long duration, imbalance and breakdown can occur, and positive influence is needed.

The peer coach can address the issues that create poor job performance or dysfunctional behaviors. Peer coaches can also assist an individual in restoring balance and harmony in their life. They include:

- Provide feedback
- Assist with problem-solving
- Assist with integration with new technology, process, and personal adaptation
- Address and assist in implementing new standards and work rules
- Assist with learning skills or procedures, upgrading of position and promotion

Peer coaches must demonstrate a trust, not carry stories back to administration, or violate that which is told to them in confidence. Peer coaches are builders, supporters and helpers. They build personal confidence and assist in bridging gaps that influence outcomes. When dealing across organizations or groups, they seek to improve collaboration and communication.

Assisting with change is an important role as well. Moving forward, meeting expectations, and being a positive influence for whatever endeavor we engage in is essential. When we encounter a roadblock or challenge having someone to assist is of great value. A peer coach brings the potential for improvement to all situations and works to make it so!

B.   A Definition of Peer Coaching[10]

Peer Coaching offers a trusting and confidential helping relationship that can assist in the following ways

- Teach others new skills
- Review and discuss assessment data
- Share ideas and resources
- Guide collaborative planning
- Expand, refine, and build new skills
- Develop and articulate change efforts
- Solve problems or address workplace challenges
- Reflect upon and analyze practices and their consequences
- Create informal assessments to measure employee performance
- Implement new strategies, including the integrated use of technology
- Examine and articulate the goal of improving practice to maximize success

Peer coaching can assist in reducing tension and mistakes, facilitate the implementation of new programs and their promotion. In effect, you are

---

[10] . www.scribd.com/doc/17065092/7-Steps-to-Building Coaching-Plan

selecting what you want to build a plan around. Whatever is decided there are similarities of need and application, the specifics inherent in the intended audience.

Table 1.
Categories for Planning Process

Individual	Occupation	Organization	Group& Community
A health issue, fiscal crisis, death in the family, loss of job, poor performance.	The workplace is moving, reduction in workforce, new supervisor, need for skills upgrading	New management, new technology, transfer, product changes, location change, etc.	Environmental, pending storm, crime issue, increased the danger, unplanned changes, etc.
1. Self-help 2. Bring order to chaos 3. New direction needed	1. Unit level 2. Division level 3. Retraining needed 4. New members to train & familiarize	1. Restructuring of jobs, implications for what you do 2. New problems to be addressed	1. Volunteers 2. Fraternal 3. Committee 4. Citizens / family / groups

Decisions to consider include:

1. What is the focus of your plan? Describe what is to be accomplished.
2. Who will be involved and why?
3. What resources will you need?

4. What is the timeframe for establishing the plan?
5. Materials needed?
6. Other specifics that are generic to your needs.

Implementing the Peer Coaching Program.

Before peer coaching can occur, a plan must be established. Peer coaching is not a single person endeavor, it must include all who will be engaged. Planning, development and putting the plans on paper is a good idea as it allows reference and review. Determining goals and the steps necessary to achieve them and ensuring it is within acceptance and achievement probabilities is also critically important. It is not a supervisor/employee arrangement, nor for the individual or group, as collaboration and communications is critical.

The peer coach establishes a positive relationship, seeks to put the individual at ease and explains that it is a collaborative relationship designed to reduce issues and increase success. The individual establishes how they will work together, who has what responsibilities and how they will communicate to ensure credibility and goal achievement.

The relationship is not one of friendship, instead of colleagues, one of whom is working to assist the other in meeting goals and expectations previously established. Decisions about communication and follow-up are made, and methods for the resolution of conflict are determined. Goals and measures to chart progress are established. Some groups may use benchmarks, and others use a tentative timeframe where a review is conducted to assess progress and to list outstanding issues. When changes or corrections in the planning process are needed, they are made.

CHAPTER Twelve
Specific Strategies to Overcome Adversity, Stress, and Trauma. Addressing Individual, Supervisor & Organization Change Efforts.

Topics Covered.

1. Connecting with others is better than isolation.
2. Flexibility is better than rigidity.
3. Communicating is better than silence.
4. We can help ourselves and others to solve problems.
5. Recognize and deal with feelings. Do not ignore them.
6. Show self-confidence and act on values, not fears.
7. Find purpose and meaning in what you do.
8. Engage in networking with others.
9. Be optimistic, not pessimistic.
10. Seek professional help.
11. Write about the issue/s.
12. Tell your story to others.
13. Use humor.
14. Take care of self.
15. Take care of others.

---

1. Connecting with others is better than isolation.

The individual.

When facing demons, it is helpful to seek out a person or persons you are comfortable with and talk out the issue and seek guidance and support.

Going it alone does not allow you the opportunity to work through issues as you tend to dwell on them, sometimes excessively. Push yourself if necessary, to talk with someone you trust and like and who will listen to your story.

Being with people you know and feel comfortable with helps diminish the negative feelings and enhances working through problems and issues.

Overcoming the depression or stress that is troubling by sharing with someone helps, can make a huge difference in your life and allows you to feel another's a helpful presence. You need to get over the "I can handle this on my own" for that does not work sometimes.

 Supervisor/Organization.

As a supervisor your responsibility is to step into the breach and address performance issues. When a subordinate is not performing as expected or his or her work is affected others the responsibility is clear. If the employee is not willing to talk with you, then explain what you are seeing, how it is harming others, and that you are eager and will assist the employee work through the issue.

If the refusal is the response and the behavior is likely to continue, then mandatory referral to EAP or another service may be the next step. The critical point, you have a responsibility to address the issue and find a resolution. This is not hard hearted; it is reaching out to help someone you have accountability with who are experiencing problems. At work, performance issues are the opening for a discussion.

And, it is also important to let the individual know that you are concerned and want to help. If you are trusted, generally good things happen.

2. Flexibility is better than rigidity.

<u>The individual.</u>

Rigid and unyielding attitude and behavior turn people off. Eventually, you will find yourself alone.

Unsmiling, griping and other negative activities are harmful to your health and to those who must deal with you.

Attempt to take a broader and more open perspective. Look for the good and not only the bad or negative. You can help your attitude by saying to yourself, "I want to feel more positive, and I will look for the good and not the negative!" Sometimes this creates a mindset that opens new feelings of optimism.

Do not seek that everything must be 100% your way or you will not participate and miss out on a lot. You might find that 60% turns out well and that you are satisfied at that level.

<u>Supervisor/Organization.</u>

With frustration comes simmering anger. When a subordinate's behavior is irritating and necessitates action, it is usually at the end of a period when you hoped the problem would resolve itself. Guard against overreaction.

When discussing an employee's behavior and its effect on the workplace, assume a more open attitude to seek understanding may open the employee to a more active partnership. When people are in a confrontational situation, it is difficult for either party not to bring up defense mechanisms. Each party tends to shut down hearing the other person. This raises the level of being "on guard" and will reduce communication.

Start from a comfortable position if possible (safety issues leave no room for negotiation) and seek the employee's compliance and weigh in problem-solving.

3. Communicating is better than silence.

The individual.

Sitting alone mulling over your problems and troubles leads to deeper levels of desperation.

Talk with people you know and respect, seek input, ask questions, find out the names of people who may be able to help.

Telling your story helps by itself, and when others weigh in, the benefit can become therapeutic.

Supervisor/Organization.

Silence, waiting for a change or facial expressions of disapproval is a waste of valuable time. Step into the breach and address the issue/s when you have enough information to make your case.

Tell the employee what you are seeing and know. Ask for their input. Seek solutions to the identified problems both from you as a supervisor and from the individual you are talking with. Their contribution is critical for it should not all come from you. Their buy-in can lead to successful change.

4. We can help ourselves and others to solve problems.

Individual

Take a piece of paper or your phone and write down the issue or problem.

Identify any variables that you feel are contributing to the issue.

Make sure you understand the situation and facts. Do not leave out an important aspect.

Make a "solutions chart" showing issues and problems and then list ways to overcome them. Be specific.

Solutions Chart

Issue or Problem	Potential Solutions	People that can help
Clearly state and define the parts. Be specific. Prioritize if it will be helpful. Provide a timeline to maintain progress.	What are probable solutions? Be open-minded as you can always cross some of them off.	List names, email addresses and telephone numbers of people who might be able to help or who can make a referral to someone who can.

1.	1.	1.
2.	2.	2.
3.	3.	3.

Frequently update your chart as new information and changes begin to take place. This can become a tracking record of how you overcame issues and problems.

Supervisor/Organization

When confronting an issue or problem it is challenging to see a solution. The power of a supervisor working with someone to find answers and to map out a path that will help resolve and reduce the trauma is critical. You must be willing and have skills appropriate to helping find a solution.

Get the employee to complete a solutions chart.

Review with him or her and add in your suggestions.

Agree with the employee on a timeframe to work on a resolution.

Conduct follow-up discussions and track progress.

5. Recognize and deal with feelings. Do not ignore them.

Individual

Keeping your feelings tightly wrapped and insulated will lead no place.

Acknowledge that you are feeling stressed, uncomfortable, edgy, and any number of other sensations. Look for them and if present acknowledge them.

Self-help may work, or it might become necessary to talk with a professional or service (EAP). There is no shame in this.

Supervisor/Organization

Getting employees to discuss feelings is difficult. It is often difficult with males and with employees of public safety organizations. Nonetheless, unless the discussion on what the employee is feeling is explored, there is little hope for resolution.

If the discussion is not working and your concern is deep enough, use the organization's policy to direct the employee to professional help.

6. Show self-confidence and act on values, not fears.

Individual

Have faith in yourself and trust your judgment.

No shortcuts. Follow straightforward self-advice.

Fear-driven decisions are often wrong as they are made in haste and without full information that is considered and weighed for accuracy.

Supervisor/Organization

Most organizations have a value statement to guide employees. The unit within which a person works or his or her immediate may also have a values statement. If one exists, it should be put on the table and discussed with the troubled employee. I also suggest doing the same with the organization's mission and goals.

See how yours and the organizations' values coincide or conflict with the individual and where adjustments are made.

Be sure to explain everything in clear terms clarifying where needed.

The goal is to give the employee confidence and to help them formulate a plan they can follow that is going to have positive results for them and the organization.

Fear of the unknown and anticipating results that may not occur can diminish the freedom to seek solutions; to reach out to bring about appropriate change. Fear paralyzes if not controlled.

7. Find purpose and meaning in what you do.

Individual

While sometimes difficult to find the motivation during times of trouble, doing something that has value to you and others that you respect and like can result in a positive pay off to you personally.

Look for the positive outcomes in what you are doing. If it helps, make a list that states the meaning of it all. Who is supported, what is the extent of that help, what can be done to make it more meaningful, etc.\Talk with others who share the work and see what their thinking is about the value in what you and they do?

Supervisor/Organization

A supervisor can help an individual explore how a job or assignment is of value and ways to find meaning in it.

This is done through discussion and questions and clearly explained and clarified answers.

Writing down key points and where issues exist allows for later clarification and resolution of contrasting points. The goal is to eliminate barriers and difficulties to the extent possible.

Renewing the employees' commitment and personal fulfillment in what they do is a positive outcome.

8. Engage in networking with others.

Individual

A powerful tool is to find others who can offer help or suggestions and who may know someone or other resources that can provide ideas and help to move you forward in meeting your goals and needs.

The more people you engage, the more significant the information and options that can lead to quality outcomes.

Supervisor/Organization

As a supervisor, you may want to assist the employee in meeting with or talking to someone who can offer insight and help.

Arrange follow-up to see that the meeting occurred. Do not inquire about the outcome unless the employee wishes to discuss.

9. Be optimistic.

Individual

Look for and see the bright side and avoid the negative that is all too easy to find. When the mind jumps to a negative response or image, stop, take a minute and ask, "what is good with what I am seeing or confronting?"

Pessimism takes valuable energy from the emotions and body and diminishes creative thinking.

Supervisor/Organization

It is not unusual for individuals experiencing difficult work conditions or stress-related trauma to embrace negativity as it helps justify already negative feelings.

Supervisors, in the discussion, should also point out the positive aspects of the situation. A crisis can be an opportunity. Seek an understanding that all is not hopeless. Look for and share information that can help and provide an uplifting experience for the employee.

10. Seek professional help.

Individual

When issues are more significant than the individual can cope with, it is essential to seek professional help from someone trained and certified.

Emotional and psychological trauma can be debilitating and harmful in many ways. Letting the symptoms persist only worsen the conditions and lead to further dysfunction.

Supervisor/Organization

Supervisors must be aware of organizational policy and services (EAP) to which an employee can be directed.

When situations persist, and additional assistance is needed, the supervisor should not hesitate to direct the employee to seek that help.

Supervisors have a responsibility to the organization and the employee, and while not always popular, appropriate action is required.

11. Write about the issue/s.

<u>Individual</u>

Writing can be therapeutic. Writing helps reduce the chaos of thinking by utilizing a more focused and linear approach to understanding what happened. Writing allows one to begin the process of mapping out where one wants to be.

Writing allows the writer to sort through and to edit and revise as the story becomes more evident. Without this, sorting out the detail is difficult when it is running in an endless loop in one's mind, causing more frustration and confusion.

Writing is a process. To understand complexity, putting it on paper and using a word processor allows a person to make distinct categories and lump like information together. Writing also allows us to note where relevant information is missing and to make notations or side notes where additional thinking must take place.

Writing for oneself is private and allows total honesty of feelings, expression of anxiety, anger, and doubt – to name a few emotions. What you may hesitate to say to others can be said in private to yourself. Reliving, considering and examining again, and seeking to make sense of something can take place as you write. You need not fear what others might think, for you are your reviewer and critic. You can best judge where you must go to bring about clarity and help with life planning.

<u>Supervisor/Organization</u>

Many of the same principles for the individual apply to the supervisor. If a situation is conflicting or confusing, it helps to write down what is known, what remains unclear or unknown and to make notes to help organize.

Supervisors can also recommend that the individual he or she is assisting write about the incident. The writer has the option to share this with the supervisor. It should be their choice.

12. **Tell your story to others.**

<u>Individual</u>

Telling one's story is commonplace with acts of heroism or extraordinary bravery or accomplishment. It allows others to share in the detail and it permits the storyteller the opportunity to not only share but process the information as it relates to one's personality, soul, and place in the world. It may well help others in their quest to seek placement in the occupation and career.

Storytelling can be entertaining, a teaching moment, a lesson on what to do or not to do and generally beneficial to the student of example and experience.

<u>Supervisor/Organization</u>

Supervisors and the organization can share relevant information with other members of the profession using the experiences of other members. A story that is well told by the person who experienced the incident or learning outcome is believable and brings grounding peer to peer.

13. Use of humor.

<u>Individual</u>

To lighten the moment is to reduce stress. When the pressure of an incident or event is oppressing, a moment of levity may shake loose the mood. We do not advocate a public display of levity, preferably a quiet and private moment of appropriate humor to break the tension. It must be done in the right frame and moment. Humor must not be executed in a demeaning manner or harm someone who is involved or present.

<u>Supervisor/Organization</u>

Supervisors have a dual role. One is to establish that humor at the expense of others is not acceptable. The other is to find humor that illustrates camaraderie and fond concern for one of their subordinates or themselves. A supervisor who can find humor reflecting some action or behavior that is relevant to them and funny can be endearing and demonstrate the level of humanness they possess.

Supervisors can use balanced self-deprecation which can be successful in stress reduction. Those that can laugh at themselves put others at ease. The balance comes in between clownish self-bashing and the act of taking oneself too seriously. And the wise supervisor will be able to strike the balance in almost all situations.

We note that humor must be tastefully done, appropriate to the moment, and not harm others. If this is accomplished correctly, it can have a positive outcome on others.

14. Take care of self.

<u>Individual</u>

Take care of your health. Eat right, exercise moderately, manage your financial health, monitor the use of alcohol and give up smoking.

Moderation is positive in our engagements.

While assistance is essential and often necessary, each person who experiences the effects of stress, adversity and trauma must self-engage in overcoming the negative impact on their emotions and physical health. Without self-engagement, any process is more difficult to assimilate into the healing process.

With the right attitude and with an optimistic outlook, it is easier to recover. Attitude and optimism are not easy at times and require grit to tough it out. Additionally, it requires a personal commitment to oneself.

<u>Supervisor/Organization</u>

Take care of yourself. The same advice reference to health, finances, and other vital aspects. Moderation also applies to the supervisor.

Supervisors also carry the responsibility to assist an employee under their charge. While this may conflict with other duty requirements, balancing the two can be accomplished. One need not compromise duty and responsibility with compassion. Understanding the dividing line and being open and honest are useful tools to use when facing this dilemma.

The organization is responsible for helping an employee who is experiencing issues and problems. The best way for this to happen is through prevention, heading off a problem before it occurs. We do not invest enough time, effort and resources to prevent employees from being overwhelmed with stress and adversity. The traditional model of "suck it up and move on" has no place in today's world where the level of trauma is often over the top. This is especially true for people working in emergency services.

15. Take care of others.

<u>Individual</u>

One of the great services you can provide to peers and other employees is to help when problems arise. Assistance must be with sincerity, honesty and without any self-aggrandizement.

If a fellow employee is sick comfort is given by merely making a call to determine how someone is feeling, if there is anything you can do to assist, run errands, and look after the needs of other family members. We often assume that when an incident is over that healing is instantaneous. This is frequently not the case! Depending on the depth of trauma, a familiar and friendly face is a vast dimension of comfort. That leads to a reduction of stress and a gradual return to health.

There have been many instances where more than one fellow employee joined together to do such chores as cut grass, go grocery shopping, help with other physical tasks that cannot be done by the injured party. A few hours of regular help reduced cost and increases feelings of well-being and removed additional worry. What a great gift!

Supervisor/Organization

The first duty of a supervisor is to care for those under his or her leadership. This means holding people to standards, to meeting the mission and goals of the agency or performing their duties in an exemplary manner. It also means that when problems arise to step up and take the lead in ensuring conditions do not get worse.

Some people who report to a supervisor may consider that individual the closest person in the organization to whom they relate. Given that, who better to step to the plate and make sure all bases are covered with the level and type of assistance needed and that includes health, domestic, property, and other influences on the life of a person who is unable to step up and care for them him or herself.

Summary.

Bringing about change and reducing contributors to stress, adversity and trauma can be addressed with the unified employee, supervisor, and organization collaboration. This requires attention to what is taking place, what are the pressure points and with that knowledge, taking steps to address them. Not all approaches work for all people.

The fifteen strategies are proven techniques that can assist in bringing about positive change. Selection of which plan to use is dependent on what preferences emerge from looking at the entire list. Resilience appears when people confront the things that create stress in their lives in a planned and organized manner.

The strategies are an overview, allowing innovation by those involved to engage in what works best for them.

CHAPTER Thirteen
Putting Peer Coaching into Practice: Stories of How it Works.

Story #1.

I was told (by long-term clients of the methadone clinic) that required counseling leaves much to be desired. It ranged from group sessions were few if any attendees talked...to playing Jenga. Jenga might be a tool for assessing five motor skills and rating dosages, but it does little to help develop the skills & attitudes necessary for sobriety.

So, I sat down with three individuals in recovery; two using methadone and one fresh out of a rehabilitation program. Using three BounceBack decks, Recovery, An Addict Among Us and the 13.5%, the individuals drew Challenges Cards from the decks and chose from the ten Skills & Attitudes they wished to apply to manage the said challenge.

The lights came on as they recognized the struggles of addiction, recovery, and poverty presented. They engaged each other by sharing their own experience and discussing the best approach (Skills & Attitudes) to use to address the issues. They asked me to add new decks noting that sobriety isn't always about managing the addiction alone. It's about managing life. – Charlene Fernald Moynihan

Their excitement was heartwarming and encouraging. The overwhelming response was.

"This is a tool that should be used during group and private counseling sessions at the methadone clinic."

"When it feels like life is generally just difficult to get through, it's hard to know what to focus on in group session. So...nothing. BounceBack could bring focus."
"I could have written this deck. This IS my life."
-Anonymous

Story #2.

A seasoned community case manager working to prevent hospitalizations for mental health clients noted:

The decks are an excellent tool for case managers. The cards create a path toward sharing, empathizing, trust, and partnership between case managers and their clients in their journey toward an improved quality of life."
-Wendy Brackett, M.H.R.T.-C, Act Team

Evaluation comments.

Used by Richard Lumb, Ph.D. to teach an online class at the University of Maine Augusta, '*Resilient and Safe Communities.*' Here's what the students had to say:

"The game is exciting and shows you how many choices you have when dealing with adversity and struggle."

"What I didn't anticipate was how easily most of the skills and attitudes would fit into each scenario."

"I played the game with my 10-year-old son, and he was able to get the concept."

"I quickly realized that I needed to emotionally invest myself into this "game" to learn something from it."

"I found that each natural disaster situation required different resilience skills. Who knew?"

"Before taking this class, I did not have a good understanding of what resilience means. It was just a buzz-word that had limited application."

"After taking this class, I can appreciate the value of a game like this. The scenarios were tough situations that happen in everyday life; we don't like to think about them."

"In each scenario, I put myself in that role and tried to make this as real life as possible to ensure that I learned something from this game."
-Anonymous

A seasoned recovery professional wrote:

"I did the Recovery cards with the guys a few days ago, and it was very well received. It opened up some great discussions."
-Adam Miller, York County Shelters Program Inc., Serenity House

An editor wrote:

"In our fast-paced world, Bounce Back provides a valuable invitation to stop and focus on how our day-to-day life choices affect both us and those in our

sphere of influence. It allows us to walk in others' shoes by opening a safe space for dialogue and insight. BounceBack is an invitation to bridge the fractures that keep us from understanding ourselves and others—that keep each and all of us from being whole."
-Wanda Whitten, Editor-in-Chief, I-DEAL WORDS Professional Editing

Our partners in France wrote:

"The ability to Bounce Back from challenge and difficulty is the behavior and attitude we all need in today's society given the continuous change and uncertainty that is part of our daily life. The work that the BounceBack team is doing has enormous potential for human empowerment. It nurtures and develops the skills required to help us deal with the unexpected and with our frustrations and perceived limitations, giving us the confidence to face our challenges and move forward.

If we were all able to bounce back in real time, we would surely live in a much more stable society where collaboration, connection, and cohesion would be the main attributes we share."-The team at PocketConfidant is proud to align and partner with BounceBack, sharing their vision and goals."
-The PocketConfidant Team

Story #3.

As I ponder my own experience with adversity, I find it is difficult to focus in on the most significant challenge of my life. Perhaps it's because life is just full of daily challenges to be managed. Maybe my years in human services has caused adversity to leave less of an impression. But I would rather think that practice managing challenges had led me to a place where I fear adversity less and respond more effectively than when I was much younger.

If I look at my occupational journey alone, I see how adversity and my response to it have changed over time. As a young person, I was both idealistic and extremely empathetic.

My very first job was at a summer recreational program for individuals with a variety of disabilities and ages. A summer camp full of happiness and fun. When a camper did not enjoy the activity planned, It was difficult for me. I had a fixed idea that summer camp was supposed to be fun for everybody. So, why did some campers resist some activities and why did some counselors push so hard for them to participate? It seemed to me, to defeat the purpose of summer camp fun. Being the introvert that I am, I did not seek out and talk with others about this, instead, I stayed inside my head trying to figure what was right. Let them choose their fun or push for participation? All the while my experience with the unhappy camper's emotions was felt in my gut.

Whether s/he was angry or panicked at being exposed to some new activity, I found myself somehow wrestling with my own emotions. It's hard to see the importance (in the moment anyway) of exposing campers to new experiences when empathy makes you feel as they do. And humor? It infuriated me when another counselor would make light of or joke about the situation. I didn't see anything funny about it.

So that's how I started my career. Not exactly the stuff of which good human service workers are made of, right? But push forward I did. I have always had a deep affection for individuals living with disabling conditions, and I continued my career working for and with these people in multiple settings. I took on progressively more challenging positions.

Ones that, at times, placed even my physical safety at risk. I developed a pattern of remaining in positions for about three to five years. From developmental day program to public school, nursing home to a hospital crisis unit, vocational rehabilitation, adult protective services, and even abuser education groups, I tested the systems.

With each new job experience, I learned (the hard way) how to manage the personal adversities that arose with my clients in more and more effective ways. I learned to connect and communicate with supervisors, co-workers, and peers for support and problem-solving. I became more open to thinking about things in a different way for the benefit of my clients; factoring in the meaning and purpose of the services provided as well as the long-term benefit to them. I gained self-confidence in my ability to manage the challenges that arose almost daily. I felt as if I were caring for others in a meaningful way.

But still, I struggled with over-empathy, my distaste for joking about things I considered too serious to joke about, and there was a little spillover of the Skills & Attitudes I had developed into my personal life. There was a consistent refrain from supervisors over the years about the need for firmer boundaries. But I had never violated any trust nor professional boundaries with any of my clients. I wasn't sure how this was to help. Because of my perspective on humor, I spent much time stuck on the negative with little relief from the emotional impact of my experiences. My personal life was a mess. And all the systems I had worked in felt broken. I was approaching burn-out.

I realized that I needed to focus more on taking care of myself if I was to be more effective with my clients and my family. I left a bad marriage and sought out those who could help me learn to care for myself with as much focus as I had cared for others. I took a step back from the job-related intensity. I took a position that offered many of the components I had always enjoyed in prior jobs but without the level of immediacy and risk should crises not be managed appropriately. I was still able to work with the population I loved and many more. It offered a sense of closure that prior jobs had not. You knew if you had performed the job correctly because the expected outcome was clear. There was enough work of abundant variety that I never found myself bored.

It was here I had space and time (18 years) to learn more of the Skills & Attitudes key to managing adversity effectively. It's not that this system was any less flawed than the others that I had worked in. But when you are exposed to a daily dose of pain, suffering, and crises, there isn't much time nor energy for learning what may be quite essential to better managing all of it. It was me that needed to change.

Today, my personal life is fulfilling despite its ongoing challenges. I am working at something I came to recognize throughout my years of service as perhaps the most critical thing that one can teach and/or learn; the Skill & Attitudes of resilience. This is what I have learned over the years:

- Systems are and will continue to be broken as long as they are underfunded, the staff is under-supported, and bureaucrats call the shots without vital knowledge of their inner workings. The best one can do is teach clients to manage some of the personal adversity that leads them to the system in the first place and how to survive that which is at times, unintentionally caused by the system and its flaws.
- Empathy brings with it additional challenges. But is not a bad quality. It offers insight into the needs of those facing some of the most intense situations. An empathic connection often leads toward a solution. Managing the related emotions, however, is key if empathy is to serve as a tool in understanding and defining the problem to be solved. Embrace empathy and work with it.
- Humor offers relief from the intensity of adversity. I remember the exact moment during a crisis that I actually laughed when a co-worker joked appropriately about the irony of a very tough situation. When I was done laughing, I felt cleansed and ready to move forward. It was the best feeling. Nobody was harmed nor offended by it. We shared a moment of relief. Turns out it's a great tool for managing adversity.

- Never let the role you play at work be the role you play at home. Home is a place of solace. It needs to be the soft place you land at the end of each day. Don't enter into relationships because they are familiar and you feel you have the skills to handle it. Family is to be loved not "handled". Care for yourself. Surround yourself with adults with whom you share a mutually supportive relationship and teach your children to be resilient and manage the inevitable adversities of life.

Some, if not all, of the ten Skills & Attitudes of resilience, can be applied to any challenge. In retrospect, I see how they could have been applied throughout my life as a tool to manage what at times seemed unmanageable. They have now been incorporated into my response repertoire. I only wish that I had learned those that I lacked at an earlier age.

Building resilience Skills & Attitudes is applicable to both personal and vocational life whether you are ten and school is the challenge or age seventy-eight and loss is the challenge. Resilience is not an innate gift nor is it difficult to learn. It's really quite simple. It just takes practice. Life is fraught with challenges and the ten Skills & Attitudes of resilience truly are "Survival Skills for the 21st. Century".
-Charlene Fernald Moynihan

Story #4. Angelica

My name is Angelica. I am 55 years old and a single mother.

In 2016 I was diagnosed with throat cancer. It is not always easy to know what to do while recovering from throat cancer. After six months of chemotherapy, I was desperate. I felt hopeless, full of fear, and lacked any vision for my future. These thoughts and feelings remained in my mind even after my chemotherapy treatment. In 2017, one year after I finished my treatment, a friend came to visit my daughter and me. He found me in a pitiful state. We had a good conversation about building resilience. We talked about how to increase resilience in situations of adversity, stress, and trauma using a tool called BounceBack. It was a great day for me.

My friend continued to visit. After several coaching sessions, I realized it was just what I needed to stand up again, recover hope, and retrieve the confidence I had lost. Those sessions changed my life dramatically. I started to communicate with others. I participated in free cancer groups, sharing information with people still in chemotherapy treatments. I began to look at the world with optimism. I took a full-time job and planned to save enough and open a small business. I was a self-employed woman in my homeland before coming to the U.S.A.

BounceBack game is definitively a tool I would recommend to those who need to boost themselves up from despair. It helped me to keep the head over the deep water at a time when I had lost all hope.
-Alphonse Ndayikengurukiye.

Story #5. B.M.M.

My name is B.M.M. I am 48 years old. I came to this country seven years ago and immediately applied for asylum. It took five years of patient waiting for my asylum to be granted. During this period I was fortunate enough to attend a resilience training session held at Hope GateWay Church in Portland ME. Dr. Ron Breazeale was the speaker. He and his team taught us about skills and attitudes to use in or order to deal with adversity in life.

I remember cold, snowy days, never seen in Africa when I was looking for someone to help me. But nobody was there. Who can help me when they cannot understand because of the language barrier; whatever I say is, "Blah, blah, blah." It is the same others speak to me. I know that every person faces their reality and I had to learn how to sustain. As an Asylum seeker working hard for little pay and not being able to get a better job, I was able to stay connected to others and live on my small budget without medical insurance. I went from one hard time to another hard time until I understood that there is another way to do things differently.

There were speeches containing lessons that went through my mind and changed the way I see challenges. The significant experience for me was that it is possible to challenge challenging situations if a person knows how to do it. There is no situation that can not be overcome if we put our attention on it and think about what to do in each case.

I learned to practice the Skills & Attitudes of BounceBack as a tool to remain balanced when facing all kinds of situations. My coach and trainer helped me to stand confidently in very complicated cases.

I practice these often to remain strong and continue my life. They are very helpful to me.

- Connect, communicate with others
- Manage strong feelings
- Self-Confidence
- See the big picture
- Care for yourself

I suggest that this game be distributed far and wide, allowing people to challenge adverse situations in our lives.
-Maurice Namwira

Story #6. M.K.

My name is M K. I am 62 years old. I attended training sessions on building resilience in Portland at Hope GateWay Church along with other immigrants and asylum seekers. The lessons learned from the training has helped me to overcome very challenging situations. I share my experience, so you can see how I used the Skills and Attitudes that I learned in my life.
I came to America in 2013 to see asylum. I faced many challenges while awaiting the issue of my application. I got my work authorization card and started working to support myself and the family I had to leave in Africa. But the long waiting time became stressful. It affected my health and my lifestyle. Learning the language alone is not easy for people of my age. I was walking in a kind of darkness.

I got a job paying $ 8.00 / hour. Without support, I had to wake up early, go to work in a cold place standing up for more than 8 hours interrupted by only small breaks. Sincerely, it was a nightmare for a person of my age. There was nobody to cares about what I was passing through. I worked so hard to assist my family back home. I was admitted to the hospital often for the care of my health. I lost my dream of joy that brought me here. I decided to quit that job and I started sewing to survive.

Far from my husband and my children, I had a sense of despair and abandonment. Day after day I asked myself why I came to this country. Working for such a low rate does not even cover my basic needs. I had no medical coverage nor money for treatment of my health problems. I had to resist and continue my life. I was able to by putting into practice the notions of resilience learned at the training session and through use of BounceBack. It helps me to sustain while I am waiting for my asylum to be granted.

These are the Skills and Attitudes I use to remain resilient:

- Connect and communicate with others
- Self-Confidence
- See the big picture

My young brother is a pastor and working with the organizers of Building Resilience training. He is my coach. I benefited from his coaching sessions to help me use those Skills and Attitudes in my daily life. In addition to the Skills and Attitudes, my trust in God has helped to overcome challenges and gives me the hope I was missing to continue my path despite the

threats and challenges of my life as an aged asylum seeker. Thank you to the initiators of these lessons. They are useful in my life.
-Maurice Namwira

APPENDIX

Toolbox of applied value for training development, planning and to assist in successful change efforts.

INDEX.

A. Strategic Planning Provides the Game Changing Events.

Richard C. Lumb

No endeavor that has a potential impact on the organization and its employees should begin without engaging in discussion and planning of what the purpose and goals are, and the sought-after outcomes Time on the front end is well spent, more comfortable to adjust, and relieves the frustrations of having to address issues during implementation.

We developed a strategic planning program for the Office of the Sheriff, Cumberland County, Maine, which was used to guide the development of the organization's plan by their officers and staff.

Strategic planning is a proactive approach to improve the organization and employee well-being.

Strategic planning demands structure as it guides and provides the pathways forward to secure what is needed to achieve the desired outcomes. Yes, it will take time, but, if at the end of the day you have the completed document in hand, you will be far along in meeting expectations.

In searching for an example to use that will assist in putting the concepts into actual dimensions that you understand was deemed critical. Most everyone has some awareness of police and first responders. Generalizing across disciplines, occupations, groups, and individual examples are more comfortable when we can compare. Thus, we use this occupational group as they too need structure, are individuals within an organization and their clients are citizens, a 360-degree service group.

Steps:

I. Mission, Goal and Objectives Statement.

Example:

1. Public Safety Planning, Policy & Research, L.L.C. (PSPP&R) and Collaborating Partners are committed to providing Peer Support Mentoring training and professional development to select Police, Fire, EMT, Correctional and other First Responder agency staff members.

> 1.2 PSPP&R in conjunction with collaborating partners will hold an assessment meeting with select target agency representatives to explore the utility and application of peer support mentors within agencies for the purposes stated. If an agreement is achieved, the parameters of a training and professional development program and corresponding evaluation would be determined.

1.3. Training instructors will be identified to conduct the training with staff supplied by the participating agencies.

> **Goal statements say where you want to be at some future time. Goals should be few, concise and not too specific. Goals indicate where the organization wants to go. A timeline is important showing milestones foraccomplishment and the beginning and ending dates.**

1.4. A series of training programs will be held, and essential agency personnel trained to the standards and outcomes determined.

1.5. A backup system for peer support mentors will be established to address the needs and problems this group encounters.

1.6. Evaluation of the peer support mentoring program will be implemented to assist as needed.

2. First responder duties and services may lead to concerns that include depression, anger, excessive absenteeism, domestic problems, hypervigilance and other behaviors that require intervention. Maintaining a confidential and trusting relationship with employees and the organization will allow the pursuit of solutions that can result in a return to balance for all involved.

2.1. Peer support mentor training will include recognizing signs and symptoms of employee disruption in the usual pattern of activity or behavior that results in conflict with organization's mission, values, rules and policy allowing them to seek intervention.

2.2. Employees experiencing self-awareness of work disruption can make the initial contact with the peer support mentor.

2.3. Peer support mentor roles include providing an open and confidential resource to the organization's employees to overcome problems and issues, before some occurrence that generally results in discipline or negative evaluation of performance.

3. Following training, peer support mentors will provide employees with prevention programs, address employee well-being needs, and conduct a proactive assessment of work conditions that can be improved.

Goal 3.1. In addition to working one-on-one with employees, the peer support mentor provides department-wide training in topics agreed on for their relevance of needs, issues, and the problems being experienced. This is a mixed growth and problem-solving service.

Goal 3.2. Peer support mentors will also maintain current knowledge of programs and support for employees that address every day and adverse situations and responses, allowing the implementation of best practices.

II. Vision Statement.

A Vision statement outlines what the organization wants to be, or how it wants the world in which it operates to be. It concentrates on the future and is a long-term view. It is a source of inspiration, provides clear decision-making criteria and gives direction to the organization's future.

Example:

The small community of Brian Ville, besieged by drug abuse resulting in the family breakup, crime, violence, and death. Police made arrests, emergency responders applied Narcan, took individuals to the hospital, and the problems seemed only to exacerbate. The Town Council was unable to devise a program, bring in sufficient assistance to decrease the issues that were ripping the community apart.

With all the chaos and seemingly endless stories of discouragement calm and clear thinking was impossible. A mental health worker in the community proposed a small group, from multiple aspects of the community, devise as a first step a vision of what they wanted to occur with the community's engagement of a strategic plan. There emerged an organized and linear approach to solutions that would be sustainable and bring order and healthy living to the inhabitants of the community.

When completed, the vision was presented, and everyone agreed it brought clarity to the fretting and emotional upheaval that existed. It allowed calmer thinking to apply and soon the process of sustainable fixes began in earnest.

III. Values Statement.

Values are the qualities that are considered worthwhile, and they represent what every employee should aspire to for priorities and which guide their actions and behaviors. They define how employees want to behave in their relationships with each other, customers, and the greater community they provide service to. They are the fundamental beliefs of people working in that organization.

We would note that values are also cultural and that sub-units of the agency also have values to their role and beliefs. The overall organization values are predominant, and no others should reduce the effectiveness of the initial statements.

Example:

We value our employees, people, partnerships, open communications, problem solving, integrity, courtesy, the Constitution of North Carolina and the Constitution of the United States.

An example from the Charlotte-Mecklenburg Police Department on the citywide application of Community Problem-Oriented Policing.

Develop Objectives

Objectives are specific, measurable targets for each goal. They are short-term and allow you to gauge the project's success. Objectives indicate what the organization expects to accomplish.

Goal 1. Strong partnerships exist among the Department, citizens, other county key businesses, other government service providers, and the private sector to enhance public safety through a balanced strategy of prevention, intervention, and enforcement. (Illustration of operations and service delivery goal)

1.2 Re-engineer all customer service processes (e.g., police, jail, document process, court protection, and other requisite services to ensure maximum customer (internal and external) satisfaction.

1.3 With the assistance of Crime and Operational Analysis, provide timely information to our problem-solving partners to facilitate and find sustainable solutions.

1.4 Work with other Key Businesses to strengthen neighborhoods, solve neighborhood problems, and increase positive contacts between the Office of the Sheriff and the communities it serves.

Action Steps

Action steps are a step-by-step process by which an organization reaches the objectives developed to fulfill the goal. They typically are programs, events, operations, and projects for the organization to accomplish its objectives. Commonly referred to as strategies.

Typically, each objective under each goal will have a series of such strategies. Action steps indicate how the organization will accomplish the goals and objectives discussed.

For example:
Goal 1: Strong partnerships exist among the Department, citizens, other county key businesses, other government service providers, and the private sector to enhance public safety through a balanced strategy of prevention, intervention, and enforcement. (Illustration of operations and service delivery goal)

> 2.1. Re-engineer all customer service processes (e.g., police, jail, document process, court protection, etc.) to ensure maximum customer (internal and external) satisfaction.

List each process (work unit) with the same objectives and determine what action steps must be taken to align them with the mission, considering the vision and values of the organization, stating specific actions steps needed to comply. Do this for each function and objective under it.

Why Strategic Planning

Strategic planning is a process that guides an organization taking charge of its future by asking the question; "Where do we want to go in the next three to five years and how will we get there"? In addition to providing a long-term organizational commitment, it provides vision and direction enabling an organization to foresee possible obstacles and difficulties. Strategic planning allows organization members to build a workable framework for internal and external responsibilities, provide services effectively and efficiently adhering to the organization's mission, vision, values, and goals.

Planning addresses collaboration guidelines with other public and private agencies and the community. Planning shapes the organization's future and permits employee input. Not having a strategic plan will result in arbitrary decisions being made that are inconsistent and not conducive to the organization itself.

The Strategic Planning Process

The strategic planning process is an important step to determine:

- What the organization is all about,
- What it wants to accomplish,
- Where it is headed,
- To establish standards of performance and behavior,
- To provide a guide for all employees to follow and provide an understanding of expectations.

Employee performance and behaviors must align with the organization's mission, vision, values, and goals. To do otherwise, we deviate from the central purpose, the reason for existence and in public service organizations, what clients expect from these services. Pulling the wagon from the front allows a vision forward, whereas pushing from the read, we only see the tailgate.

The decision to take this step rests with the chief executive who must communicate his or her commitment and convey the importance of the process. This action is not an option, it will get done, and it will serve as a guide to employees on conducting the organization's business.

Table 1

Planning Process.

Mission, Vision, Values, Goals, Objectives, Action Steps.

Recommended 8 Step Process

1. The decision to Proceed.
2. Member Notification and Buy-in
3. Organize/Planning Process decisionmaking. (1st) Group Meeting.
4. Development Mission, Vision, Values.
5. Goal Statements. (2nd) Group Meeting)
6. Develop Objectives.
7. Final Draft Manual.
8. Acceptance and Use of Plan. Third (3rd) & Final Group Meeting.

Timeline Chart

Steps with Timeline to Complete
1. Decision to Proceed
2. Notifications
3. Organize to plan
4. Mission, vision, values
5. Goals
6. Objectives
7. Final Draft
8. Acceptance

Step #1: Decision to Proceed.

Activity	Timeframe
1. Chief executive officer decides to proceed. It is suggested that an in-depth discussion occur, or a small group be tasked with addressing the below areas. The purpose is to put all members on the same page of understanding, and that will help keep an appropriate focus on the task at hand. Considerations: 1.1. Organization Assessment. 1.1.2. Identify and list all customer service processes that are provided by the organization. 1.1.3. Identify essential customer services provided. 1.1.4. What are the organization's strengths, Weaknesses, Opportunities, and Threats internally and externally?	Dates:

1.1.5. What are the Political, Economic, Social, and Technology influences on the agency and how are they being managed? 1.1.6. What are the socio-cultural, regulatory, environmental, information, social and legal issues facing the organization in carrying out its duties and responsibilities?
The purpose of the assessment is to take an inventory of the organization, a current snapshot so that when developing the strategic plan takes place, pressures, demands, and regulatory influences on the organization are understood. The plan must be realistic as the "ideal" may not be possible at this stage. Provide an accurate summary to assist in the development of the strategic plan.

Step #2: Member Notification and Buy-in.

Activity	Timeframe
2. Staff and employees/members notified of the decision. This is a significant undertaking, a step that will define who, what, why and when the organization will engage in the business it champions. It is preferable that	Dates:

people associated understand and are willing to participate in the change process.	

Step #3: Organize/Planning Process decisionmaking.

First (1st) Group Meeting.

Activity	Timeframe
3. Schedule first meeting - To reaffirm commitment and review what will take place. 3.1 Important to discuss the process of plan development and the steps involved. 3.2 Expectations of the planning group for outcomes and use of a plan. 3.3 The steps in plan development. A plan reflects organization mission, vision, values, goals and action steps, as such, it emerges from the group, not supplied to them by an outside consultant, but facilitated and guided with essential support and assistance. 3.4 What the consultant proposes to ensure completion of the plan. 3.5 Determine sub-committee assignments, reporting, and work to be done. Sub-committees have an essential role and include inquiry and communications. 3.6 A tentative timetable for completion.	Dates:

3.7 <u>The facilitator</u> is present and distributes a strategic planning workbook. 3.7.1 Explain the planning process. 3.7.2 Discussion sub-committee assignments. 3.7.3 Discuss reporting and distribution roles. 3.7.4 Editing and recommendations for emerging work. 3.7.5 Establish meeting times and dates.	

Step #4: Development Mission, Vision, Values.

Activity	Timeframe
This step is accomplished by individuals selected or volunteers to a sub-committee of each component.	
4. Develop <u>Mission</u>, <u>Vision</u>, and <u>Values</u> Statements. <ul><li>Assignment of members to three sub-committees.</li><li>These members will work collaboratively to develop their assignments, distribute to others and facilitator for edits and recommendations.</li><li>The mission, vision, and values statements are critical and establish the foundation for all other components.</li></ul><u>Step #1</u>. Mission statement sub-committee draft developed.	Dates:

Step #2. Vision statement sub-committee draft developed. Step #3. Values statement sub-committee draft developed. 4.1. Establish a date when the full group reviews and finalizes the work of the three sub-committees. 4.2. Alternative means of review to a group meeting can be developed 4.2.1 and include the following: Technology exchange, analysis, and input. 4.2.2 A smaller group is designated to meet and finalize the information. Distribution and final input by total membership may be obtained electronically.	

Step #5: Goal Statements. (Second (2nd) Group Meeting)

Activity	Timeframe

5. Develop organization goal statements. The mission, vision, and values statements are completed before this step.
    A. Facilitator review, explanation and example of:
    • What goals and objectives are and their "fit" to mission, vision, and values.
    • How they are defined and developed.
	Dates:

B. Discuss goal categories, if they are to be used or receive a group decision on what the format will be. • Management and Organizational • Operations and Service Delivery • Human Resources • Technology • Facilities 5.1. Goals sub-committee develops the draft document. • Work and collaborate as needed to create goal statements using categories is determined. • Facilitator to assist with edits recommendations and submissions of personal thoughts. 5.2. At the completion of the sub-committee work, the goals are distributed to the full group for review and edit. 5.3. Recommendations are sent to the Sub-committee chair for finalization. The facilitator will assist as needed.	

Step #6: Develop Objectives.

Activity	Timeframe
6. Develop objectives for each of the final goals. 6.1. Sub-committees are formed and assigned one or more goals. These groups will develop objectives under each of the goals. • The facilitator will forward an objective development training guide and will assist any of the sub-committees with this step as needed. 6.2. As objectives are developed, an oversight sub-committee can be appointed <u>and</u> the facilitator to clarify language and intent. • Draft goals and objectives will be sent electronically, clearly labeled as to draft date and number, to all members for input and edit 6.3. At an estimated date, a document containing mission, vision, values, goals and objectives will be sent to all members for review and edit. At the end of this process that material can be approved and finalized. We are 85 percent complete. • The next step is to include action steps, if elected to be done, including them under each of the objectives.	Dates:

Action steps include assignments and timelines. • Recommended the same sub-committee members serve on the development of action steps. 6.4. Draft objectives and action steps will be sent electronically, clearly labeled as to draft. They are sent to all group members for input and edit.	

Step #7. Final Draft Manual.

Activity	Timeframe
7. When all parts are completed, a strategic planning manual will be drafted. • Sent to all members for final review and input. • Any comments are sent to the oversight committee. • Final changes made	Dates:

Step #8. Acceptance and Use of Plan.
Third (3rd) & Final Group Meeting.

Activity	Timeframe
8. The full group accepts strategic planning manual. • A discussion on its use. • Implementation	Dates:

• Measuring effectiveness and recording notes for incorporation into a revision in 3 or 5 years. This might include the appointment of an oversight manager, someone to keep records, to initiate reminders, to ensure that the plan is being implemented.	

Workbook to Guide the Planning Process:
Mainewoods Education and Training
Richard C. Lumb, Ph.D.
Wilton, Maine

B. Strategic Personal Coaching
Rita Schiano

Strategic personal coaching is a more targeted form of life coaching that utilizes the skills and attitudes of resilience to provide new perspectives and recommend strategies for people looking to make changes in their personal or professional life.

Strategic personal coaching is customized to the individual's most important goals, interests, challenges, and needs. The purpose of strategic personal coaching is to offer insight and assistance that will guide the person towards actionable, positive changes that will affect all areas of the person's life.

Throughout the coaching process, the coach and individual will explore the long-standing attitudes and habits that have influenced the person's life, what I call habitudes. To begin the process, the coach explains how at an early age we developed emotional habits and patterns -- habitudes -- that influence how we perceive and move through our lives. These often unconscious, persistent ways of thinking and acting shape one's narrative.

As William James wrote in 1892, "All our life, so far as it has definite form, is but a mass of habits." And while most of the choices we make each day may feel like the products of well-considered decision making, they are not. They are habits. More than forty percent of the actions we perform each day aren't actual decisions; they're habits. (Duke University study referenced by Charles Duhigg, *The Power of Habit,* 2012) Some habits serve us; others do not. This notion goes back even further in time, to Aristotle circa 330

B.C. Regardless, these habits determine many of the outcomes in our lives.

Habits aren't destiny. Patterns are the choices that all of us deliberately make at some point, and then stop thinking about but continue doing, often every day. Behavior became automatic (organizational habits). It's a natural consequence of our neurology. Once an addiction manifests, the brain stops fully participating in the decision-making. That's why people addicted to cell phones will text while driving.

Habits that don't serve us, keep us stuck in negative, dysfunctional, reactive-responsive patterns.
When you have a habit that you have reinforced for months or years, that habit is a connection to your nervous system.

We must create new neurological routines that overpower those behaviors and take control of the habit loop. Habits can change if we understand how they work. One way we do this is by learning to observe the cues and rewards so that we can change the routines.

Individuals and habits are all different, and so the specifics of recognizing, understanding, and changing the patterns in our lives differ from person to person and behavior to behavior. Giving up cigarettes is different from curbing overeating, which is different from changing how you communicate with your spouse, which is different from how you prioritize tasks at work.
Therefore people are not successful at breaking a habit. Can't "Just Stop." Not that simple. What's

more, each person's habits are driven by different cravings — physical, emotional. (Smell triggers emotion more than any other of the five senses.)

Habits never really disappear. They are encoded into the structures of our brain, and that's a massive advantage for us (e.g., riding a bike).

The problem is that your mind can't tell the difference between bad and good habits. We must learn to create new neurological routines that overpower those behaviors — take control of the habit loop.

So how do we change these habitudes that do not serve us? How do we make the shift towards positive thoughts and actions? By exploring, breaking down, and understanding the habitude process and uncovering one's resilient skills and attitudes, the building blocks to strengthening and maintaining one's resiliency. If you can follow the thinking that drives your emotions, you can change the meaning (you created) and change your behavior.

Armed with this insight, you as coach will guide the person in developing a workable plan to manage the challenges that come his or her way.

The process of strategic personal coaching reinforces the resilience skills and attitudes that individuals have and develops the ones needed to help them achieve their goals and meet the challenges they may encounter along the way.

Depending on the individual's interests, goals and needs, strategic personal coaching can focus on one or more of these areas:

- **Career coaching** -- Advance in one's career and transition to a new job.
- **Personal and professional development** -- Focuses on helping the person perform and execute better at work
- **Health and wellness** -- Breaking down the habits that serve the individual and the practices that don't; exploring and explaining how stress affects his or her health; focus on building resilience skills and attitudes
- **Interpersonal relationships** -- Improving communication, conflict and emotional intelligence to enhance one's relationship skills
- **Work/life balance** -- Establishing healthy boundaries between work and personal life
- **Achieving success** -- Developing the skills, mindsets, and strategies needed to succeed and achieve their goals

Strategic Personal Coaching is a process, and the duration of the coaching relationship varies depending on one's personal preferences and needs.

C. Holmes and Rahe Self-Test Stress Scale.

The Holmes and Rahe Stress Scale is a list of 43 stressful life events that can contribute to an individual's illness. In 1967, Psychiatrists Thomas Holmes and Richard Rahe examined the medical records of over 5,000 medical patients to determine whether stressful events might cause illness. Patients were asked to tally a list of 43 life events based on a relative score. A positive correlation of 0.118 was found between their life events and their illnesses.

Their results were published as the Social Readjustment Rating Scale (SRRS), known more commonly as the Holmes and Rahe Stress Scale. Subsequent validation has supported the links between stress and illness.

Supporting Research

Rahe carried out a study in 1970 testing the reliability of the stress scale as a predictor of illness. The scale was applied to 2,500 US sailors, and they were asked to rate scores of 'life events' over the previous six months. Over the next six months, detailed records kept of the sailors' health. There was a +0.118 correlation between stress scale scores and illness, which was enough to support the hypothesis of a link between life events and illness. In conjunction with the Cornell Medical Index Assessing, the stress scale correlated with visits to medical dispensaries, and the H&R stress scale's scores also correlated independently with individuals dropping out of stressful underwater demolitions training due to medical problems. The scale was also assessed against different populations within the United States (with African, Hispanic and White American groups). The scale was also tested cross-culturally, comparing Japanese and Malaysian groups with American populations.

Adults

To measure stress according to the Holmes and Rahe Stress Scale, the number of "Life Change Units" that apply to events in the past year of an individual's life were added to the final score and will give a rough estimate of how stress affects health.

Non-adults

A modified scale has been developed for non-adults. Like the adult scale, stress points for life events in the past year added and compared to the rough estimate of how stress affects health.

Note:

This process is not a test that provides "absolute" outcomes; rather it is a general concept self-examination that you can take, or give to others, to determine where stressors lie for the individual. It can be a guide to help you consider "next steps" if you are feeling stressed and uncomfortable.

Place a check mark next to any descriptor you have in your life, add the total points, and check the last box to get a general overview of the depth or level of stress you might be feeling.

Holmes and Rahe Stress Scale Study - Categories and Point Value

Adults	Pts	Non-Adults	Pts
1. Death of a spouse	100	Getting married	101
2. Divorce	73	Unwed pregnancy	92
3. Marital separation	65	Death of parent	87
4. Imprisonment	63	Acquiring a visible deformity	81
5. Death of a close family member	63	Divorce of parents	77
6. Personal injury or illness	53	Fathering an unwed pregnancy	77
7. Marriage	50	Becoming involved with drugs or alcohol	76
8. Dismissal from work	47	Jail sentence of a parent for over one year	75
9. Marital reconciliation	45	Marital separation of parents	69
10. Retirement	45	Death of a brother or sister	68
11. Change in health of a family member	44	Change in acceptance by peers	67
12. Pregnancy	40	Pregnancy of unwed sister	64
13. Sexual difficulties	39	Discovery of being an adopted child	63
14. Gain a new family member	39	The marriage of parent to step-parent	63
15. Business readjustment	39	Death of a close friend	63
16. Change in financial state	38	Having a visible congenital deformity	62
17. Change in frequency of arguments	35	Serious illness requiring hospitalization	58

18. Major mortgage	32	Failure of a grade in school	56
19. Foreclosure of mortgage or loan	30	Not making an extracurricular activity	55
20. Change in responsibilities at work	29	Hospitalization of a parent	55
21. Child leaving home	29	Jail sentence of a parent for over 30 days	53
22. Trouble with in-laws	29	Breaking up with boyfriend or girlfriend	53
23. Outstanding personal achievement	28	Beginning to date	51
24. Spouse starts or stops work	26	Suspension from school	50
25. Begin or end school	26	Birth of a brother or sister	50
26. Change in living conditions	25	Increase in arguments between parents	47
27. Revision of personal habits	24	Loss of job by the parent	46
28. Trouble with boss	23	Outstanding personal achievement	46
29. Change in working hours or conditions	20	Change in parent's financial status	45
30. Change in residence	20	Accepted at a college of choice	43
31. Change in schools	20	Being a senior in high school	42
32. Change in recreation	19	Hospitalization of a sibling	41

33. Change in church activities	19	The increased absence of a parent from home	38
34. Change in social activities	18	Brother or sister leaving home	37
35. Minor mortgage or loan	17	Addition of the third adult to family	34
36. Change in sleeping habits	16	Becoming a full-fledged church member	31
37. Change in number of family reunions	15	The decrease in arguments between parents	27
38. Change in eating habits	15	The decrease in arguments with parents	26
39. Vacation	13	Mother or father beginning work	26
40. Christmas	12		
41. Minor violation of the law	11		
Adult Scores: 1. >300 At the risk of illness 2. 150-229 Risk of illness is moderate[11] 3. <150 Slight risks of illness		Non-adult Scores: 1. >300 At the risk of illness 2. 150-299 Risk of illness is moderate[1] 3. <150 Slight risks of illness	

I. Perceived Stress Self-Test[12].

---

[11] . A 30% reduction from #1.

[12] .

http://faculty.weber.edu/molpin/healthclasses/1110/bookchapters/selfassessmentchapter.htm

The Perceived Stress Scale (PSS) is a classic stress assessment instrument. This tool, while initially developed in 1983, remains a popular choice for helping us understand how different situations affect our feelings and our perceived stress.

The questions in this scale ask about your feelings and thoughts during the last month. In each case, you will be asked to indicate how often you felt or thought a certain way. Although some of the questions are similar, there are differences between them, and you should treat each one as a separate question. The best approach is to answer quickly. That is, don't try to count the number of times you felt a particular way; instead, indicate the alternative that seems like a reasonable estimate. This self-test provides only an indicator and should be considered empirical in outcomes.

<u>For each question choose from the following:</u>

       0 – Never
       1 - Almost never
       2 – Sometimes
       3 – Fairly often
       4 – Very often

Place a check mark in the column box most representing your response to the question.

Self-assessment Question	0	1	2	3	4
1. In the last month, how often have you been upset because of something that happened unexpectedly?					

2. In the last month, how often have you felt that you were unable to control the essential things in your life?					
3. In the last month, how often have you felt nervous and stressed?					
4. In the last month, how often have you felt confident about your ability to handle your problems?					
5. In the last month, how often have you felt that things were going your way?					
6. In the last month, how often have you found that you could not cope with all the things that you had to do?					
7. In the last month, how often have you been able to control irritations in your life?					
8. In the last month, how often have you felt that you were on top of things?					
9. In the last month, how often have you been angered because of things that happened that were outside of your control?					
10. In the last month, how often have you felt difficulties were piling up so high that you could not overcome them?					

Figuring your PSS score:

You can determine your PSS score by following these directions:

1. First, reverse your scores for questions 4, 5, 7, & 8. On these 4 questions, change the scores like this: 0 = 4, 1 = 3, 2 = 2, 3 = 1, 4 = 0.

Nbr	Pg. 1 Original Score	Adjusted Score
1		
2		
3		
4		
5		
6		
7		
8		
9		
10		
TOT	XXXXX	

2. Now add up your scores for each item to get a total.

My total score is _____.

Individual scores on the PSS can range from 0 to 40 with higher scores indicating higher perceived stress.

Scores ranging from 0-13 would be considered low stress.
Scores ranging from 14-26 would be considered moderate stress.
Scores ranging from 27-40 would be considered high perceived stress.

Resources:

Ronald. L. Breazeale, Ph.D.,
https://2050ceanavenue.com/therapist-directory/ronald-breazeale/,
http://www.abilitycoach.com/about.html

Psychological and Educational Services, Portland
https://2050ceanavenue.com/
Building Resilience, L.L.C., Founder
https://building-resilience.com/

Building Resilience, L.L.C., http://building-resilience.com, https://building-resilience.ecwid.com/

We provide resilience training and tools to individuals and communities that wish to promote independent management of adversity and problem-solving among their members. We work together with those who desire to create an atmosphere of peer support and mentoring within their communities.

The focus of our training is on personal resilience because that is where the learning must start. When large groups of individuals develop resilience Skills & Attitudes, communities can be strengthened. Abundant research supports the affirmation that resilient individuals are the building blocks of resilient communities. It is our goal to build resilient communities; one individual at a time.

Our training can be customized to focus on specific challenges using topic presented in our BounceBack decks. It can be generic using a mix of selections from our decks. Or, we can work with the issues relevant to and provided by our community. Individuals are most engaged by challenges they can relate to. We are willing and prepared to work with you to customize our training to meet the needs of your community.

If your community would benefit from training contact c.fernaldmoynihan@building-resilience.com.

Richard C. Lumb, Ph.D.,
https://www.linkedin.com/in/richard-lumb-549b9227

Public Safety Planning, Policy and Research, L.L.C., http://rclumb.blogspot.com/
 Maine Woods Training and Education Services, https://sites.google.com/site/mainewoodseducation/

PSPP&R, LLC and Maine Woods Training & Educational Services provides hands-on service to organizations and groups to address persistent problems leading to sustainable solutions. Additionally, we conduct professional development and train-the-trainer services in (a) Resilience, (b) Sustainable Community Capacity Building, (c) Program Development and Evaluation, (d) Substance Abuse Interventions (with Colleague from SUNY Brockport, NY, (e) Advanced Individual and Organizational Leadership Roles, and, Assist organizations develop sustainable community and stakeholder collaborative partnerships.

PocketConfidant, https://pocketconfidant.com/

Do you ever feel stuck? Would you like to make better decisions or prioritize. Do you need a "sounding board" to test your thinking?

PocketConfidant is a self-coaching tool (a conversational technology with a robot-coach) to help you formulate your thoughts and challenges in real-time. Guiding you to clarify your own thinking, identify your precise needs, resources and goals, formulate your outcome or intention and envision what you want to do next.

Individuals, managers, leaders, team members all benefit by supporting themselves and each other to increase their personal capacity for self-reflection, decision-making, prioritization, goal-setting, communication and confidence.

Research tells us that coaching is an invaluable tool for developing people across a wide range of needs. The benefits of coaching are many; 80% of people who receive coaching report increased self-confidence, and over 70% benefit from improved work performance, relationships, and more effective communication skills. (source: ICF 2009).

With PocketConfidant, access a private and confidential place to talk. Conversations are depersonalized and encrypted so that individuals' privacy is protected at all times. No individual or group will ever see or know the contents of another's conversation without their explicit consent. The goal is not to replace a human professional but provide the mechanisms that support each individual when they need it.

For more information contact hello@pocketconfidant.com.

Rita Schiano, M.A.,

http://www.ritaschiano.com/

Rita Schiano is a resilience strategist and coach, speaker, and founder of Rita Schiano ~ Live A Flourishing Life. A former corporate vice-president and small business owner, Rita's leadership knowledge, strategies, and insights draw from both sides of the aisle. Organizations use Rita to help staff build resilient leadership skills, manage stress, and improve morale. As a personal strategic coach, Rita helps clients focus specifically on their most important goals, interests, challenges, and needs. The goal of private sessions is to offer insight and assistance that guides you towards actionable, positive changes that will affect all areas of your life. Rita received her Strategic Intervention Coaching Certificate from Robbins-Madanes.

She is the author of several books, including Live A Flourishing Life, a stress management and resilience-building process workbook; the critically-acclaimed, semi-autobiographical novel Painting The Invisible Man, and Sweet Bitter Love and articles for The Huffington Post / AOL Healthy Living, the Worcester Business Journal, and guest blogger for Psychology Today.

For a list of our programs and workshops, visit http://www.ritaschiano.com/category/Programs-Workshops-/c51. For more information on Strategic Personal Coaching, please contact Rita directly at http://www.ritaschiano.com/.

Made in the USA
Middletown, DE
23 July 2019